A GUIDE

TO THE

PRE-CIVIL WAR LAND RECORDS

OF

COLLETON COUNTY SOUTH CAROLINA

Carroll Ainsworth McElligott
and Ronald J. McElligott II

HERITAGE BOOKS
2025

HERITAGE BOOKS
AN IMPRINT OF HERITAGE BOOKS, INC.

Books, CDs, and more—Worldwide

For our listing of thousands of titles see our website
at
www.HeritageBooks.com

A Facsimile Reprint
Published 2025 by
HERITAGE BOOKS, INC.
Publishing Division
5810 Ruatan Street
Berwyn Heights, MD 20740

Copyright © 2000 Carroll Ainsworth McElligott
and Ronald J. McElligott II

— Publisher's Notice —
In reprints such as this, it is often not possible to remove blemishes from the original. We feel the contents of this book warrant its reissue despite these blemishes and hope you will agree and read it with pleasure.

International Standard Book Number
Paperbound: 978-0-7884-1607-1

Contents

Introduction   vii

Abstracts of Land Records Executed Prior to
    1 January 1866 from the Direct Index
    to Deeds, 1865-1974, Colleton County,
    South Carolina   3

Glossary   97

Grantee Index   101

Introduction

The records of the Colleton County, South Carolina, Courthouse were destroyed during the Civil War. After the War, many documents pertaining to land transactions that date prior to the Civil War were recorded or re-recorded and are on file in the Office of the Clerk of Court, Colleton County Courthouse, Walterboro, South Carolina. This work is a summary of the information contained in these documents.

Within these one hundred thirty pages, six hundred ninety-four names are listed as grantors; and four hundred fifty names are listed as grantees.

The information found in the *Direct Index to Deeds, 1865-1974, Colleton County, South Carolina* is of great importance to the genealogist and historian studying pre-Civil War South Carolina. Each of the following abstracts contains the name of grantor, name of grantee, date the instrument was recorded or re-recorded, book and page number where the instrument is recorded, kind of instrument, and description of property. Information not available in the *Direct Index* is indicated by three dashes (---).

"Abstracts of Land Records Executed Prior to 1 January 1866 from the Direct Index to Deeds, 1865-1974, Colleton County, South Carolina" is arranged alphabetically by grantor and is followed by a glossary and a grantee index.

Names appear as spelled in the *Direct Index*. In some instances, we have compared the names in the *Direct Index* to those in the original documents and have indicated the differences that we have found. We have used the more common spelling of Salkahatchie throughout this document, although it is spelled various ways in the *Direct Index*.

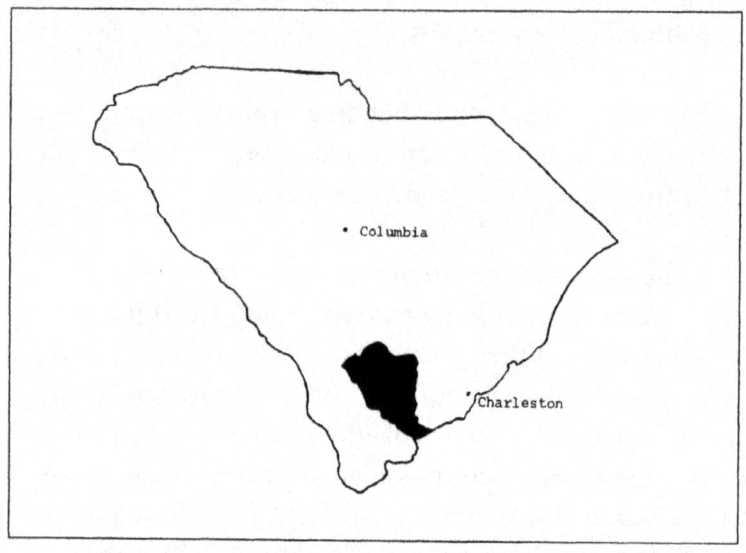

Map of South Carolina showing the
location of Colleton County as it existed at
the time of the subject records.

A Guide to the Pre-Civil War Land Records of Colleton County, South Carolina

Abstracts of Land Records Executed Prior to 1 January 1866 from the Direct Index to Deeds, 1865-1974

Abstracts of Land Records
Executed Prior to 1 January 1866
from the Direct Index to Deeds,
1865-1974, Colleton County, South Carolina

Ackerman, D. S. H., Grantor; Lawrence B. Ackerman, Grantee; Date of instrument: 1854; Date of record: 24 Sept. 1870; Book D, Page 338; Kind of instrument: Title; Description of property: 550 acres on South side of Edisto River.

Ackerman, Edwin M., Grantor; Stephen O. Ackerman, et al, Grantee; Date of instrument: 1848; Date of record: 24 Sept. 1870; Book D, Page 337; Kind of instrument: Title; Description of property: Near Maple Cane.

Ackerman, H. W., Grantor; Richard Risher, Grantee; Date of instrument: 2 Apr. 1855; Date of record: 24 Sept. 1870; Book D, Page 341; Kind of instrument: Title; Description of property: On Horse Pen Bay, St. Bar. Par.

Aiken, Wm., Grantor; Alfred P. Walker, Grantee; Date of instrument: 2 Mar. 1846; Date of record: 24 Feb. 1897; Book 16, Page 557; Kind of instrument: Grant; Description of property: St. Bar. Par.

Allen, Mary L., Grantor; E. S. P. Bellinger, Grantee; Date of instrument: 1 July 1845; Date of record: 13

Oct. 1922; Book 52, Page 424; Kind of instrument: Conv.; Description of property: 1200 acres of land more or less.

Allen, Mary L., Grantor; M. E. Carn, Grantee; Date of instrument: 26 June 1845; Date of record: 13 Oct. 1922; Book 52, Page 421; Kind of instrument: Power of atty.; Description of property: ---.

Allen, Mary, et al, Grantor; J. W. Green, et al, Grantee; Date of instrument: 12 Jan. 1848; Date of record: 14 Apr. 1892; Book 13, Page 225; Kind of instrument: Petition for title; Description of property: ---.

Alston, Thos. Pinckney, et al (by M. E.), Grantor; Benj. Burgh Smith, Grantee; Date of instrument: 1 Nov. 1859; Date of record: 8 June 1869; Book C, Page 180; Kind of instrument: Conv.; Description of property: Wilderness on Caw Caw Swamp.

Anderson, Isaac S., Grantor; Henry W. Lucken, Grantee; Date of instrument: 31 Oct. 1863; Date of record: 1 June 1866; Book A, Page 94; Kind of instrument: T.R.E.; Description of property: Lot in Walterboro.

Ashe, Chas. C., et al (by C. E.), Grantor; Isham Lowrey, Grantee; Date of instrument: 19 Aug. 1836; Date of record: 13 July 1883; Book 1, Page 271; Kind of instrument: Conv.; Description of property: On Horse Shoe Creek.

Ashe, John S., Ex'or (by M. E.), Grantor; John S. Ashe, Grantee; Date of instrument: 26 Feb. 1833; Date of record: 6 Mar. 1879; Book 0, Page 56; Kind of instrument: T.R.E.; Description of property: Walnut Hill, St. Paul's Par.

Ashe, John S., Grantor; Thos. Y. Simmons, Grantee; Date of instrument: 17 May 1832; Date of record: 6 May 1879; Book 0, Page 57; Kind of instrument: Title; Description of property: Walnut Hill, St. Paul's Par.

Atkinson, James, Grantor; Ann Hickman, Grantee; Date of instrument: 14 Jan. 1854; Date of record: 21 Dec. 1883; Book 1, Page 471; Kind of instrument: T.R.E.; Description of property: Portion of Grant to Robertson tract.

Bailey, James, et al, Grantor; James Bailey, Jr., Grantee; Date of instrument: 25 Apr. 1857; Date of record: 23 Sept. 1901; Book 21, Page 64; Kind of instrument: T.R.E.; Description of property: On Little Salkahatchie.

Bailey, James, Grantor; Richard Bailey, Grantee; Date of instrument: 25 Apr. 1857; Date of record: 13 Feb. 1920; Book 48, Page 534; Kind of instrument: T.R.E.; Description of property: 208 acres.

Beach, Abram, Grantor; Lewis O'Bryan, Grantee; Date of instrument: 13 Oct. 1857; Date of record: 21 Aug. 1868; Book B, Page 414; Kind of instrument: Title; Description of property: 254 acres on Round O.

Beach, John H., et al, Grantor; Lewis E. Linder, Grantee; Date of instrument: 7 Dec. 1865; Date of record: 15 Oct. 1917; Plat Book, 249; Kind of instrument: ---; Description of property: On and between Jones Swamp and Wolf Creek.

Beach, N. W., Grantor; William Spell, Grantee; Date of instrument: 6 Dec. 1858; Date of record: 4 Feb. 1871; Book E, Page 23; Kind of instrument: T.R.E.; Description of property: On Wolf Creek Waters of Combahee.

Bell, Catharine C., et al, Grantor; David Givens, Grantee; Date of instrument: 1 Dec. 1860; Date of record: 19 July 1912; Book 36, Page 262; Kind of instrument: T.R.E.; Description of property: On Indian Creek.

Bell, J. W., et al, Grantor; David Givens, Grantee; Date of instrument: 1 Dec. 1860; Date of record: 19 July 1912; Book 36, Page 262; Kind of instrument: T.R.E.; Description of property: On Indian Creek.

Bell, Jas. S., et al, Grantor; David Givens, Grantee; Date of instrument: 1 Dec. 1860; Date of record: 19 July 1912; Book 36, Page 262; Kind of instrument: T.R.E.; Description of property: On Indian Creek.

Bell, John, et al (by heirs), Grantor; David Givens, Grantee; Date of instrument: 1 Dec. 1860; Date of record: 19 July 1912; Book 36, Page 262; Kind of instrument: T.R.E.; Description of property: On Indian Creek.

Bell, John, Grantor; Mary Murdaugh, Grantee; Date of instrument: 8 Feb. 1858; Date of record: 19 Mar. 1885; Book 2, Page 548; Kind of instrument: T.R.E.; Description of property: On Great Salkahatchie.

Bell, John, Grantor; T. A. Bootle, Grantee; Date of instrument: 3 Dec. 1856; Date of record: 28 July 1866; Book A, Page 150; Kind of instrument: T.R.E.; Description of property: 92 acres on Elbow Branch.

Bell, Julia A., et al, Grantor; David Givens, Grantee; Date of instrument: 1 Dec. 1860; Date of record: 19 July 1912; Book 36, Page 262; Kind of instrument: T.R.E.; Description of property: On Indian Creek.

Bell, Rebecca, et al, Grantor; David Givens, Grantee; Date of instrument: 1 Dec. 1860; Date of record: 19 July 1912; Book 36, Page 262; Kind of instrument: T.R.E.; Description of property: On Indian Creek.

Benton, Job, et al (by Sh'ff), Grantor; Wm. Washington Benton, et al, Grantee; Date of instrument: 6 Dec. 1852; Date of record: 3 Oct. 1870; Book D, Page 345; Kind of instrument: Title; Description of property: On Black Creek.

Benton, Job, Grantor; R. W. Benton, Grantee; Date of instrument: 17 July 1855; Date of record: 16 Feb. 1867; Book A, Page 389; Kind of instrument: Conv.; Description of property: Spring Hill tract on Black Creek.

Benton, Joshua, Grantor; E. C. C. G. M. Hudson, Grantee; Date of instrument: 10 Jan. 1855; Date of record: 2 Nov. 1881; Book T, Page 76; Kind of instrument: Conv.; Description of property: On Black Creek.

Benton, Samuel, Grantor; Allen Gwens, et al, Grantee; Date of instrument: 18 July 1850; Date of record: 21 Jan. 1880; Book O, Page 447; Kind of instrument: Title; Description of property: St. Bartholomew's Parish.

Black, John, et al (Wardens), Grantor; Edwin Walker, Grantee; Date of instrument: 19 Jan. 1857; Date of record: 18 Sept. 1905; Book 27, Page 131; Kind of instrument: Timber sale; Description of property: On Sandy Run & Bull Branch.

Black, Martha, et al (wardens), Grantor; Edwin Walker, Grantee; Date of instrument: 19 Jan. 1857; Date of record: 18 Sept. 1905; Book 27, Page 131; Kind of instrument: Timber sale; Description of property: On Sandy Run & Bull Branch.

Blake, Daniel, Grantor; A. McB. Peeples, Grantee; Date of instrument: 1 Feb. 1861; Date of record: 4 Feb. 1873; Book G, Page 200; Kind of instrument: T.R.E.; Description of property: On waters of Salkahatchie River.

Blocker, John, Grantor; R. B. Beach, Grantee; Date of instrument: 19 Jan. 1857; Date of record: 16 Aug. 1899; Book 19, Page 329; Kind of instrument: T.R.E.; Description of property: North by lands of L. E. Linder, et al.

Blocker, John, Grantor; R. B. Beach, Grantee; Date of instrument: 2 May 1853; Date of record: 4 Nov. 1867; Book B, Page 18; Kind of instrument: Conv.; Description of property: On Jones Swamp 198 acres.

Blocker, John, Grantor; Wesley Beach, Grantee; Date of instrument: 23 Jan. 1858; Date of record: 17 Dec. 1878; Book J, Page 567; Kind of instrument: Title; Description of property: On Jones Swamp.

Blocker, John, Grantor; William Carter, Grantee; Date of instrument: 22 Sept. 1865; Date of record: 11 Mar. 1915; Book 41, Page 249; Kind of instrument: Conv.; Description of property: On Wolf Creek.

Boatwright, L. B., Grantor; Mary Preacher, Grantee; Date of instrument: 1 Nov. 1865; Date of record: 19 Mar. 1867; Book A, Page 489; Kind of instrument: T.R.E.; Description of property: St. Bar. Parish on Indian Creek.

Borck, Moses, Grantor; Gustave Jacoby, Grantee; Date of instrument: 30 Dec. 1864; Date of record: 6 June 1868; Book B, Page 312; Kind of instrument: Conv.; Description of property: 100 acres St. Bar. Parish.

Bowman, James, Grantor; Frederick Fraser, Grantee; Date of instrument: 1 Feb. 1828; Date of record: 8 June 1868; Book B, Page 317; Kind of instrument: Conv.; Description of property: On Horse Shoe Creek.

Bowman, Thos., Grantor; W. C. Hazel, Grantee; Date of instrument: 1 June 1841; Date of record: 5 Apr. 1909; Book 25, Page 495; Kind of instrument: Plat; Description of property: On Middle Swamp Waters of Stono River.

Bowman, Thos., Grantor; Wm C. Hazel, Grantee; Date of instrument: 15 Apr. 1853; Date of record: 5 Apr. 1909; Book 28, Page 452; Kind of instrument: Deed; Description of property: St. Paul's Par. on Middle Swamp.

Boynton, Stephen, et al, Grantor; T. J. D. Hiott, Grantee; Date of instrument: Nov. 1859; Date of record:

30 Jan. 1926; Book 58, Page 196; Kind of instrument: T.R.E.; Description of property: Near Sandy Dam Church.

Bray, Catherine C., et al, Grantor; A. McB. Peeples, Grantee; Date of instrument: 1 May 1857; Date of record: 5 July 1887; Book 6, Page 34; Kind of instrument: T.R.E.; Description of property: Red Hill Tract & Cross Roads Tract.

Bray, Charles, et al, Grantor; A. McB. Peeples, Grantee; Date of instrument: 1 May 1857; Date of record: 5 July 1887; Book 6, Page 34; Kind of instrument: T.R.E.; Description of property: Red Hill Tract & Cross Roads Tract.

Bryan, Edward, Grantor; E. H. Bryan, Grantee; Date of instrument: 29 June 1836; Date of record: 15 Oct. 1866; Book A, Page 216; Kind of instrument: T.R.E.; Description of property: East side of Little Salkahatchie.

Bryan, Edward, Grantor; Edward H. Bryan, Grantee; Date of instrument: 18 Feb. 1850; Date of record: 15 Oct. 1866; Book A, Page 217; Kind of instrument: T.R.E.; Description of property: On waters of Salkahatchie.

Bunting, E. M., Grantor; H. A. Gibson, Grantee; Date of instrument: 3 Aug. 1859; Date of record: 14 Feb. 1890; Book 9, Page 271; Kind of instrument:

T.R.E.; Description of property: Bounded by Adams, et al.

Bunting, Owen, Sr., Grantor; Lewis O'Bryan (Trs), Grantee; Date of instrument: 31 Aug. 1854; Date of record: 2 Mar. 1870; Book D, Page 10; Kind of instrument: Trust Deed; Description of property: Several tracts.

Burbidge, J. W., et al (Admr) (by C. E.), Grantor; Isaac Sauls, Grantee; Date of instrument: 4 Oct. 1852; Date of record: ---; Book C, Page 346; Kind of instrument: T.R.E.; Description of property: St. Paul's Par., Walnut Hill Tract.

Burbidge, Jno. W., Exor, Grantor; Sampson L. Paul, Grantee; Date of instrument: 6 Jan. 1859; Date of record: 26 May 1886; Book 4, Page 192; Kind of instrument: T.R.E.; Description of property: Lot in Walterboro.

Burbidge, John W., et al, Grantor; Jno. M. Stanfield, Grantee; Date of instrument: 6 Mar. 1854; Date of record: 19 Mar. 1884; Book 2, Page 95; Kind of instrument: T.R.E.; Description of property: On Round O at Irons Cross Roads.

Burbidge, John W., Exor, Grantor; Jas. L. Paul, Grantee; Date of instrument: 7 Feb. 1857; Date of record: 26 May 1886; Book 4, Page 188; Kind of instrument: T.R.E.; Description of property: In Walterboro.

Burbidge, John W., Grantor; Benj. Johnson, Grantee; Date of instrument: 31 July 1856; Date of record: 21 Feb. 1908; Book 29, Page 570; Kind of instrument: T.R.E.; Description of property: St. Bar. Parish.

Burnett, A. W., Grantor; T. B. Clarkson, Grantee; Date of instrument: ---; Date of record: 21 Sept. 1871; Book E, Page 302; Kind of instrument: Levy on realty; Description of property: On Combahee River.

Burnett, Andrew W., Grantor; Emanuel Witsell, Grantee; Date of instrument: 27 Sept. 1859; Date[1] of record: ---; Book D, Page 248; Kind of instrument: Title; Description of property: On Pon Pon River.

Burnett, Andrew W., Grantor; James Lynah, et al, Grantee; Date of instrument: Nov. 1835; Date of record: 6 Feb. 1869; Book B, Page 618; Kind of instrument: Marriage settlement; Description of property: St. Bar. Parish.

Burns, James D., Grantor; L. W. McCants (Trs), Grantee; Date of instrument: 30 Aug. 1852; Date of record: 19 July 1884; Book 1, Page 610; Kind of instrument: T.R.E.; Description of property: On Horse Shoe.

Butler, P. M., Grantor; David Smoke, Grantee; Date of instrument: 6 Aug. 1838; Date of record: ---;

Book I, Page 607; Kind of instrument: T.R.E.; Description of property: On Buckhead & Bear Branch.

Campbell, A., (C. E.), Grantor; Sampson L. Paul, et al, Grantee; Date of instrument: 11 Feb. 1845; Date of record: 26 May 1870; Book D, Page 156; Kind of instrument: Title; Description of property: On Horse Shoe Creek.

Campbell, A., et al, Grantor; Edmond B. Platt, Grantee; Date of instrument: 1 Apr. 1850; Date of record: 17 Oct. 1877; Book J, Page 181; Kind of instrument: Title; Description of property: St. Paul's Parish.

Campbell, A., Grantor; Jas. Bowman, Grantee; Date of instrument: 4 Feb. 1836; Date of record: 3 June 1889; Book 8, Page 127; Kind of instrument: T.R.E.; Description of property: Lots in Walterboro.

Campbell, Arch'd L., et al, Grantor; Laurence W. McCants, Grantee; Date of instrument: 31 May 1847; Date of record: 30 Sept. 1871; Book E, Page 317; Kind of instrument: Marriage settlement; Description of property: St. Bar. Parish.

Campbell, Archibald, (C. E.), Grantor; Maria Glover, Grantee; Date of instrument: 18 Dec. 1846; Date of record: 26 Mar. 1891; Book 10, Page 319;

Kind of instrument: T.R.E.; Description of property: River Place, et al.

Campbell, Archibald, (C. E.), Grantor; R. M. Touchstone, Grantee; Date of instrument: 14 Mar. 1846; Date of record: 21 Sept. 1870; Book D, Page 321; Kind of instrument: Title; Description of property: On South side of Edisto River.

Campbell, Archibald, (C. E.), Grantor; Wm. Pottell, Grantee; Date of instrument: 1 Jan. 1844; Date of record: 26 Mar. 1886; Book 4, Page 190; Kind of instrument: T.R.E.; Description of property: In Walterboro.

Campbell, James B., Grantor; Edward Caleb, et al, Grantee; Date of instrument: 19 Mar. 1858; Date of record: 18 Nov. 1885; Book 3, Page 43; Kind of instrument: T.R.E.; Description of property: St. Paul's Parish, Johnstone.

Campbell, Mary B., et al, Grantor; Laurence W. McCants, Grantee; Date of instrument: 31 May 1847; Date of record: 30 Sept. 1871; Book E, Page 317; Kind of instrument: Marriage settlement; Description of property: St. Bar. Parish.

Campbell, Wm. L., Grantor; G. W. Oswald, Grantee; Date of instrument: 11 Feb. 1861; Date of record: 26 Mar. 1889; Book 8, Page 8; Kind of instrument: T.R.E.; Description of property: In Walterboro.

Canady, S. B., Grantor; O. B. T. Canady, Grantee; Date of instrument: 2 Dec. 1852; Date of record: 23 Apr. 1885; Book 1, Page 745; Kind of instrument: T.R.E.; Description of property: In Walterboro.

Canady, T. D., (by Exors), Grantor; Moses Hodge, Grantee; Date of instrument: 10 Aug. 1860; Date of record: 20 Jan. 1882; Book T, Page 188; Kind of instrument: Conv.; Description of property: Old House Tract, et al.

Cannaday, Jane W., (Ex ix) et al, Grantor; Moses Hodge, Grantee; Date of instrument: 10 Aug. 1860; Date of record: 20 Jan. 1882; Book T, Page 188; Kind of instrument: Conv.; Description of property: Old House Tract, et al.

Carn, M. E., Grantor; R. W. Chaplin, Grantee; Date of instrument: 7 June 1853; Date of record: 31 Apr. 1870; Book D, Page 302; Kind of instrument: Title; Description of property: St. Paul's Parish.

Carn, M. E., Grantor; S. B. Cannady, Grantee; Date of instrument: 15 Dec. 1849; Date of record: 10 Feb. 1888; Book 6, Page 206; Kind of instrument: T.R.E.; Description of property: In Walterboro.

Carson, H. W., Grantor; Henry Crosby, Grantee; Date of instrument: 3 Dec. 1865; Date of record: 13 Dec. 1902; Book 23, Page 21; Kind of instrument: Conv.; Description of property: North by lands of Reuben Stephens.

Carter, Eleanor, Grantor; M. P. Vaughn, Grantee; Date of instrument: 21 June 1859; Date of record: 27 Dec. 1867; Book B, Page 79; Kind of instrument: Conv. in trust; Description of property: On Little Salkahatchie River.

Carter, Henry O., Grantor; Dempsey Conoly, Grantee; Date of instrument: 1 Dec. 1859; Date of record: 8 Feb. 1912; Book 36, Page 12; Kind of instrument: T.R.E.; Description of property: On Little Salkahatchie.

Carter, Wm. P., Grantor; Joel Padgett, Grantee; Date of instrument: 9 Aug. 1861; Date of record: 8 Dec. 1913; Book 38, Page 329; Kind of instrument: T.R.E.; Description of property: On or near Little Salkahatchie.

Chamberlin, Charles V., Grantor; George N. Miller, Grantee; Date of instrument: 10 Feb. 1865; Date of record: 14 Aug. 1877; Book J, Page 130; Kind of instrument: Dec of uses; Description of property: Various tracts.

Chaplin, Wm. W., Grantor; R. W. Chaplin, Grantee; Date of instrument: 4 July 1853; Date of record: 31 Aug. 1870; Book D, Page 303; Kind of instrument: T.R.E.; Description of property: St. Paul's Parish.

Clarke, T. A. G., Admr., Grantor; Chas. & Sav. R. R. Co., Grantee; Date of instrument: 31 Jan. 1860; Date of record: 24 Nov. 1916; Book 43, Page 518; Kind of instrument: Deed; Description of property: ---.

Clement, M. W., Grantor; Luder F. Behling, Grantee; Date of instrument: 15 June 1862; Date of record: 1 Feb. 1872; Book F, Page 3; Kind of instrument: Conv.; Description of property: St. Paul's Parish.

Clement, W. W., Grantor; Luder F. Behling, Grantee; Date of instrument: 14 Sept. 1855; Date of record: 24 Apr. 1888; Book 7, Page 199; Kind of instrument: T.R.E.; Description of property: Known as Flinn's.

Clifford, L. C., et al, Grantor; B. L. Risher, et al, Grantee; Date of instrument: 3 Aug. 1857; Date of record: 11 Nov. 1905; Book 24, Page 524; Kind of instrument: T.R.E.; Description of property: On Edisto River.

Colliers, Edward, Grantor; James Grimes, Grantee; Date of instrument: 1 May 1863; Date of record: 28 Aug. 1899; Book 19, Page 338; Kind of instrument: T.R.E.; Description of property: St. Paul's Parish.

Colson, Mary, et al (by Sh'ff), Grantor; Alex Stephens, Grantee; Date of instrument: 29 Dec. 1855; Date of record: 8 June 1885; Book 2, Page 650; Kind of instrument: T.R.E.; Description of property: St. Bar. Parish.

Cone, Andrew, Grantor; Richard Hiers, Grantee; Date of instrument: 13 Mar. 1857; Date of record: 23 Sept. 1885; Book 2, Page 743, Kind of instrument: T.R.E.; Description of property: On Waters of Salkahatchie.

Coone, John, et al, Grantor; Trustees Tabor Church, Grantee; Date of instrument: 28 July 1840; Date of record: 15 Feb. 1941; Book 80, Page 63; Kind of instrument: Deed; Description of property: 2 acres 1 road.

Cordray, David, Grantor; Wm. H. Nix, et al, Grantee; Date of instrument: July 1863; Date of record: 5 Mar. 1869; Book C, Page 121; Kind of instrument: Deed in Trust; Description of property: On Round O.

Cordray, Thomas, Grantor; R. W. Chaplin, Grantee; Date of instrument: 6 Mar. 1858; Date of record: 10 June 1867; Book A, Page 608; Kind of instrument: T.R.E.; Description of property: Known as Log Bridge Tract on Wilton Road.

Corrie, William C., Grantor; Priscilla C. Ferguson, Grantee; Date of instrument: 16 Aug. 1859; Date of record: 9 Nov. 1909; MRE Book 32, Page 63; Kind of instrument: T.R.E.; Description of property: In Walterboro.

Crosby, Henry, Grantor; Henry E. Crosby, Grantee; Date of instrument: 5 Mar. 1845; Date of record: 28

Feb. 1870; Book C, Page 503; Kind of instrument: T.R.E.; Description of property: 500 acres on waters of Packers Bay.

Crosby, J. M., (by Sh'ff), Grantor; I. M. Crosby, Sr., Grantee; Date of instrument: 5 Mar. 1855; Date of record: 3 Jan. 1870; Book C, Page 423; Kind of instrument: T.R.E.; Description of property: St. Bar. Parish.

Crosby, Jacob, (by sh'ff), Grantor; Robert Padgett, Grantee; Date of instrument: 22 Nov. 1848; Date of record: 29 Apr. 1870; Book , Page 240; Kind of instrument: Title; Description of property: 100 acres on Salkahatchie.

Dandridge, John, Grantor; Chas. E. Koger, Grantee; Date of instrument: 1 Jan. 1844; Date of record: 21 Nov. 1918; Book 47, Page 420; Kind of instrument: T.R.E.; Description of property: 211 acres more or less.

Davis, C. I., Grantor; J. S. Hickman, Grantee; Date of instrument: 14 Nov. 1865; Date of record: 3 Jan. 1870; Book C, Page 426; Kind of instrument: T.R.E.; Description of property: Near Walterboro.

Davis, C. J., Grantor; C. J. D. Marsh, Grantee; Date of instrument: 8 Jan. 1856; Date of record: 18 Feb. 1873; Book G, Page 227; Kind of instrument: T.R.E.; Description of property: On Old Field Creek.

Davis, Chas. I., Grantor; Solomon Harris, Grantee; Date of instrument: 23 Dec. 1863; Date of record: 11 Sept. 1877; Book J, Page 154; Kind of instrument: Title; Description of property: Part of Johnson Lands.

Davis, Nathan, Grantor; Moses Borck, Grantee; Date of instrument: 6 Sept. 1864; Date of record: 6 June 1868; Book B, Page 311; Kind of instrument: Conv.; Description of property: 100 acres, St. Bar. Parish.

Dent, E. A., Grantor; Alexander Robertson, Grantee; Date of instrument: 18 Dec. 1846; Date of record: 13 Aug. 1908; Plat Book, Page 110; Kind of instrument: Plat; Description of property: ---.

DeSaussure, Louis D., Grantor; Henry Bischoff, Grantee; Date of instrument: 19 Dec. 1822; Date of record: 15 Jan. 1873; Book G, Page 179; Kind of instrument: T.R.E.; Description of property: On Waters of Pon Pon River.

Devant, R. I., (C. E.), Grantor; Richard Freeman, Grantee; Date of instrument: 1 June 1835; Date of record: 10 June 1867; Book A, Page 603; Kind of instrument: Conv. in fee; Description of property: St. Paul's Parish.

DeWitt, James, Grantor; M. S. Thompson, Grantee; Date of instrument: 28 Sept. .1860; Date of record: 3 Oct. 1892; Book 12, Page 329; Kind of instrument: Conv.; Description of property: On Waters of Ashepoo River.

Dopson, E. H., et al, Grantor; William Walker, Grantee; Date of instrument: 20 Apr. 1850; Date of record: 16 Dec. 1871; Book E, Page 368; Kind of instrument: T.R.E.; Description of property: On McCunes Branch.

Dopson, Martha A., et al, Grantor; William Walker, Grantee; Date of instrument: 20 Apr. 1850; Date of record: 16 Dec. 1871; Book E, Page 368; Kind of instrument: T.R.E.; Description of property: On McCunes Branch.

Drawdy, Jas., et al (by Sh'ff), Grantor; O. P. Williams, Grantee; Date of instrument: 5 July 1861; Date of record: 15 Mar. 1880; Book P, Page 152; Kind of instrument: T.R.E.; Description of property: St. Bar. Par.

DuBois, J. A. A., (Admr.) (by C. E.), Grantor; C. I. Davis, Grantee; Date of instrument: 15 Mar. 1858; Date of record: 3 Jan. 1870; Book C, Page 424; Kind of instrument: T.R.E.; Description of property: Near Walterboro.

Edwards, Jno. D., Grantor; O. T. Cannady, Grantee; Date of instrument: 2 Dec. 1853; Date of record: 28 Jan. 1884; Book 1, Page 527; Kind of instrument: Title; Description of property: In Walterboro.

Elliott, Thos. O., (M. E.), Grantor; John S. Ashe, Grantee; Date of instrument: 26 Feb. 1833; Date of record: 6 Mar. 1879; Book O, Page 56; Kind of instrument: Title; Description of property: Walnut Hill, St. Paul's Parish.

England, Alexander, et al (Exors), Grantor; John T. Marshall, Grantee; Date of instrument: 5 Nov. 1847; Date of record: 11 Jan. 1876; Book I, Page 477; Kind of instrument: T.R.E.; Description of property: St. Paul's Parish.

English grant, Grantor; Edward Fenwick, Grantee; Date of instrument: 29 Mar. 1754; Date of record: 9 June 1964; Plat Box, Page 220A; Kind of instrument: Plat; Description of property: Est Edward Fenwick.

Ex Parte, Grantor; (Dr.) Alexander Fraser, Grantee; Date of instrument: 20 Mar. 1816; Date of record: 8 June 1868; Book B, Page 314; Kind of instrument: Plat; Description of property: On Horse Shoe Creek.

Ex Parte, Grantor; (Dr.) Peter Stokes, Grantee; Date of instrument: 19 Oct. 1865; Date of record: 29 Apr. 1867; Book A, Page 591; Kind of instrument: Plat; Description of property: On Edisto River Swamp.

Ex Parte, Grantor; (Dr.) Peter Stokes, Grantee; Date of instrument: 5 Oct. 1865; Date of record: 29 Apr.

1867; Book A, Page 590; Kind of instrument: Plat; Description of property: House Tract on Edisto River Swamp.

Ex Parte, Grantor; Benj'm L. Risher, Grantee; Date of instrument: 22 Dec. 1854; Date of record: 11 Feb. 1937; Book 3, Page 5; Kind of instrument: Plat; Description of property: 381 acres.

Ex Parte, Grantor; Charles Baring, Grantee; Date of instrument: 2 Dec. 1850; Date of record: 27 July 1866; Book A, Page 142; Kind of instrument: Plat; Description of property: On Pon Pon in St. Paul's Parish.

Ex Parte, Grantor; Elijah Benton, Grantee; Date of instrument: 13 Mar. 1802; Date of record: 21 July 1919; Plat Book, Page 332; Kind of instrument: Plat; Description of property: ---.

Ex Parte, Grantor; Jas. S. Glover, et al, Grantee; Date of instrument: ---; Date of record: ---; Book B, Page 510; Kind of instrument: Petition & Testimony; Description of property: On Horse Shoe.

Ex Parte, Grantor; Jas. S. Glover, et al, Grantee; Date of instrument: ---; Date of record: ---; Book B, Page 511; Kind of instrument: Petition & Testimony; Description of property: "Hards" on Horse Shoe.

Ex Parte, Grantor; Joseph Fraser, Grantee; Date of instrument: 20 Mar. 1816; Date of record: 8 June

1868; Book B, Page 315; Kind of instrument: Plat; Description of property: On Horse Shoe Creek.

Ex Parte, Grantor; Peter Stokes, Grantee; Date of instrument: 17 Oct. 1865; Date of record: 29 Apr. 1867; Book A, Page 592; Kind of instrument: Plat; Description of property: Near Buck Head.

Ex Parte, Grantor; Peter Stokes, Grantee; Date of instrument: 25 Oct. 1865; Date of record: 29 Apr. 1867; Book A, Page 581; Kind of instrument: Plat; Description of property: 800 acres on Bear Branch on Salkahatchie River.

Ex Parte, Grantor; Peter Stokes, Grantee; Date of instrument: 4 Oct. 1865; Date of record: 29 Apr. 1867; Book A, Page 589; Kind of instrument: Plat; Description of property: Called May Swamp near Edisto River.

Ex Parte, Grantor; Susan Snipe, Grantee; Date of instrument: 2 Oct. 1863; Date of record: 9 Dec. 1905; Plat Book, Page 82; Kind of instrument: Plat; Description of property: On Round O.

Ex Parte, Grantor; William Newton, Grantee; Date of instrument: 1 Feb. 1860; Date of record: 11 Dec. 1905; Plat Book, Page 83; Kind of instrument: Plat; Description of property: St. Paul's Parish.

Ex Parte, Grantor; William P. Carter, Grantee; Date of instrument: 6 Mar. 1861; Date of record: 8 Dec. 1913; Book 39, Page 319; Kind of instrument: Plat; Description of property: On or near Little Salkahatchie Swamp.

Ex Parte, Grantor; William Wilkie, Grantee; Date of instrument: 25 May 1825; Date of record: 18 Apr. 1967; Book 12, Page 61; Kind of instrument: Plat; Description of property: 221 acres.

Farmer, C. B., (C. E.), Grantor; B. S. Rivers, Grantee; Date of instrument: 11 June 1862; Date of record: 17 July 1882; Book T, Page 727; Kind of instrument: Deed; Description of property: Lot #63 in Walterboro.

Farmer, C. B., (C. E.), Grantor; C. I. Davis, Grantee; Date of instrument: 15 Mar. 1858; Date of record: 3 Jan. 1870; Book C, Page 424; Kind of instrument: T.R.E.; Description of property: Near Walterboro.

Farmer, C. B., (C. E.), Grantor; C. I. Davis, Grantee; Date of instrument: 15 Mar. 1858; Date of record: 3 Jan. 1870; Book C, Page 424; Kind of instrument: T.R.E.; Description of property: Near Walterboro.

Farmer, C. B., (C. E.), Grantor; Carlos Tracy, Grantee; Date of instrument: Oct. 1858; Date of record: 30 July 1890; Book 8, Page 497; Kind of instrument: T.R.E.; Description of property: In Walterboro.

Farmer, C. B., (C. E.), Grantor; John Bell, Grantee; Date of instrument: 4 Apr. 1859; Date of record: 3 Jan. 1870; Book C, Page 437; Kind of instrument: T.R.E.; Description of property: Formerly of Harper & Verdier.

Farmer, C. B., (C. E.), Grantor; John Hanckell, Grantee; Date of instrument: 5 June 1863; Date of record: 21 Mar. 1866; Book A, Page 92; Kind of instrument: T.R.E.; Description of property: Pocosabo & Lining Tracts, et al.

Farmer, C. B., (C. E.), Grantor; John Hanckell, Grantee; Date of instrument: 5 June 1863; Date of record: 21 Mar. 1866; Book A, Page 92; Kind of instrument: T.R.E.; Description of property: Pocosabo & Lining Tracts, et al.

Farmer, C. B., (C. E.), Grantor; L. W. McCants, Grantee; Date of instrument: 27 Jan. 1859; Date of record: 12 Jan. 1874; Book G, Page 615; Kind of instrument: T.R.E.; Description of property: On Round O.

Farmer, C. B., Grantor; John Bell, Grantee; Date of instrument: 4 Apr. 1859; Date of record: 3 Jan. 1870; Book C, Page 437; Kind of instrument: T.R.E.; Description of property: Formerly of Harper & Verdier.

Farmer, C. Baring, Grantor; J. J. Klein, Grantee; Date of instrument: 18 Nov. 1859; Date of record: 17

June 1869; Book C, Page 197; Kind of instrument: T.R.E.; Description of property: In Walterboro.

Farmer, C. Baring, Grantor; J. J. Klein, Grantee; Date of instrument: 18 Nov. 1859; Date of record: 17 June 1869; Book C, Page 197; Kind of instrument: T.R.E.; Description of property: In Walterboro.

Farmer, C. E., (C. E.), Grantor; L. W. McCants, Grantee; Date of instrument: 27 Jan. 1859; Date of record: 12 Jan. 1874; Book G, Page 615; Kind of instrument: T.R.E.; Description of property: On Round O.

Fender, J. J., Grantor; J. W. Fender, Grantee; Date of instrument: 18 Aug. 1859; Date of record: 16 Feb. 1869; Book C, Page 19; Kind of instrument: T.R.E.; Description of property: On Green Pond Road.

Fogler, Jasper, et al, Grantor; John J. Fender, Grantee; Date of instrument: 29 Oct. 1851; Date of record: 8 Sept. 1879; Book 0, Page 241; Kind of instrument: Conv.; Description of property: On Savannah Creek.

Fogler, Susan C., et al, Grantor; John J. Fender, Grantee; Date of instrument: 29 Oct. 1851; Date of record: 8 Sept. 1879; Book 0, Page 241; Kind of instrument: Conv.; Description of property: On Savannah Creek.

Ford, Malachi, (Admr.), Grantor; Simon Verdier, Grantee; Date of instrument: ---; Date of record: 22 June 1870; Book D, Page 197; Kind of instrument: Title; Description of property: "Brown Tract."

Ford, Malachi, (C. E.), Grantor; Daniel Warren, Grantee; Date of instrument: 5 Apr. 1824; Date of record: 8 Mar. 1877; Book J, Page 28; Kind of instrument: Title; Description of property: 428 acres on Buckhead.

Ford, Malachi, (C. E.), Grantor; F. Y. Glover, Grantee; Date of instrument: 20 Feb. 1829; Date of record: 12 Dec. 1867; Book B, Page 55; Kind of instrument: Title; Description of property: In Walterboro.

Ford, Malachi, (C. E.), Grantor; Isham Lowrey, Grantee; Date of instrument: 19 Aug. 1836; Date of record: 13 July 1883; Book 1, Page 271; Kind of instrument: Conv.; Description of property: On Horse Shoe Creek.

Ford, Malachi, (C. E.), Grantor; Jacob Stevens, Grantee; Date of instrument: 16 Mar. 1829; Date of record: 21 Jan. 1887; Book 5, Page 162; Kind of instrument: T.R.E.; Description of property: In Walterboro.

Ford, Malachi, (C. E.), Grantor; Jane May, Grantee; Date of instrument: 8 May 1832; Date of record: 17 May 1889; Book 8, Page 102; Kind of instrument: T.R.E.; Description of property: In Walterboro.

Ford, Malachi, Grantor; Elijah Benton, Grantee; Date of instrument: 4 Nov. 1837; Date of record: 19 Sept. 1905; Book 27, Page 118; Kind of instrument: T.R.E.; Description of property: On Salkahatchie.

Ford, Malachi, Grantor; Chas. S. Stokes, et al, Grantee; Date of instrument: 11 Feb. 1833; Date of record: 13 Mar. 1931; Book 65, Page 477; Kind of instrument: T.R.E.; Description of property: ---.

Fraser, Frederick, Grantor; F. W. Fraser, Grantee; Date of instrument: 24 Jan. 1857; Date of record: 20 Mar. 1868; Book B, Page 264; Kind of instrument: Conv.; Description of property: In Walterboro.

Fraser, Joseph, Grantor; Frederick Fraser, Grantee; Date of instrument: 28 Dec. 1822; Date of record: 8 June 1868; Book B, Page 312; Kind of instrument: Release; Description of property: At Horse Shoe.

Freeman, Jas. W., (by Trus. et al), Grantor; R. W. Chaplin, Grantee; Date of instrument: 10 July 1856; Date of record: 10 June 1867; Book A,

Page 604; Kind of instrument: Conv.; Description of property: St. Paul's Parish.

Freeman, M. N., (Trs.), Grantor; R. W. Chaplin, Grantee; Date of instrument: 10 July 1856; Date of record: 10 June 1867; Book A, Page 604; Kind of instrument: Conv.; Description of property: St. Paul's Parish.

Fripp, Clarence A., Grantor; A. J. Salinas, Grantee; Date of instrument: 20 Oct. 1863; Date of record: 18 Sept. 1866; Book A, Page 192; Kind of instrument: T.R.E.; Description of property: St. Paul's Par.

Fripp, James T. E., et al, Grantor; Joel Larisey, Grantee; Date of instrument: 28 Apr. 1863; Date of record: 18 Mar. 1867; Book A, Page 580; Kind of instrument: Deed; Description of property: On Waters of Ashepoo River.

Fripp, P. H., et al, Grantor; Joel Larisey, Grantee; Date of instrument: 28 Apr. 1863; Date of record: 18 Mar. 1867; Book A, Page 580; Kind of instrument: Deed; Description of property: On Waters of Ashepoo River.

Furman, C. M., (M. E.), Grantor; S. W. Leith, Grantee; Date of instrument: 1 Feb. 1831; Date of record: 26 May 1870; Book D, Page 153; Kind of instrument: Title; Description of property: On Chuckessee Creek.

Furman, Chas. M., Grantor; Chas. Baring, Grantee; Date of instrument: 22 Mar. 1832; Date of record: 5 Apr. 1879; Book O, Page 101; Kind of instrument: Conv.; Description of property: St. Paul's Par.

Garris, Elvina, Grantor; B. W. Garris, Grantee; Date of instrument: 28 July 1846; Date of record: 25 July 1879; Book 0, Page 184; Kind of instrument: Deed; Description of property: On Little Salkahatchie.

Garvin, T. A., Grantor; Henry Kinsey, Grantee; Date of instrument: 24 Feb. 1855; Date of record: 7 Oct. 1897; Book 16, Page 732; Kind of instrument: Conv.; Description of property: On Little Salkahatchie.

Gest, Wm. H., Grantor; Edward Colliers, Grantee; Date of instrument: 10 Feb. 1860; Date of record: 28 Aug. 1899; Book 19, Page 338; Kind of instrument: Conv.; Description of property: St. Paul's Par.

Getsinger, Jacob, Grantor; J. G. A. DuBois, Grantee; Date of instrument: 6 Jan. 1860; Date of record: 9 Nov. 1868; Book C, Page 268; Kind of instrument: Conv.; Description of property: On Little Salkahatchie.

Getsinger, W. C., Grantor; James Corbett, Grantee; Date of instrument: 26 Aug. 1861; Date of record: 8

Jan. 1886; Book 3, Page 139; Kind of instrument: T.R.E.; Description of property: Part of Wilson Land.

Getsinger, Wm., Grantor; Henry Varnado, Grantee; Date of instrument: 24 Nov. 1863; Date of record: 12 Feb. 1880; Book O, Page 496; Kind of instrument: Deed; Description of property: Bounded by Stephens, et al.

Gibbes, W. H., (Mas.), Grantor; Wm. Greenwood, Grantee; Date of instrument: 5 Apr. 1810; Date of record: 21 July 1891; Book 11, Page 384; Kind of instrument: T.R.E.; Description of property: On Edisto.

Gibson, H. A., Grantor; J. J. Getsinger, Grantee; Date of instrument: 16 June 1863; Date of record: 14 Feb. 1890; Book 9, Page 272; Kind of instrument: T.R.E.; Description of property: On Waters of Great Swamp.

Glover, Eliza, et al, Grantor; J. Edward Glover, Grantee; Date of instrument: 11 Apr. 1856; Date of record: 27 Oct. 1866; Book A, Page 223; Kind of instrument: Conv. in Fee; Description of property: Near Walterboro.

Glover, Eliza, Grantor; J. Edward Glover, Grantee; Date of instrument: Sept. 1853; Date of record: 15 Feb. 1867; Book A, Page 408; Kind of instrument: Conv.; Description of property: Near Walterboro.

Glover, Eliza, Grantor; Thomas Pye, Grantee; Date of instrument: 11 July 1856; Date of record: 24 Jan. 1871; Book D, Page 500; Kind of instrument: Conv.; Description of property: 265 acres, St. Bar. Parish.

Glover, F. Y., (Dr.), Grantor; (Dr.) J. Edward Glover, Grantee; Date of instrument: 27 July 1840; Date of record: 12 Dec. 1867; Book B, Page 58; Kind of instrument: Title; Description of property: In Walterboro.

Glover, Francis Y., Grantor; J. Edward Glover, Grantee; Date of instrument: 6 June 1844; Date of record: 12 Dec. 1867; Book B, Page 60; Kind of instrument: Title; Description of property: In Walterboro.

Glover, H. C., Grantor; David Cordry, Grantee; Date of instrument: 12 Mar. 1863; Date of record: 28 June 1869; Book C, Page 307; Kind of instrument: T.R.E.; Description of property: In Round O.

Glover, Harriett, et al, Grantor; Dan'l H. Silcox (Trs.), Grantee; Date of instrument: 4 Feb. 1858; Date of record: 6 Sept. 1888; Book 6, Page 451; Kind of instrument: T.R.E.; Description of property: Near Jacksonboro.

Glover, J. Cart., Grantor; Eliza Glover, Grantee; Date of instrument: 19 Jan. 1856; Date of record: 18 June

1894; Book 14, Page 520; Kind of instrument: T.R.E.; Description of property: In Walterboro.

Glover, J. Cart., Grantor; Josiah Beck, Grantee; Date of instrument: 17 Apr. 1852; Date of record: 1 June 1868; Book B, Page 304; Kind of instrument: Title; Description of property: "Boundary Farm" near Parkers Ferry.

Glover, J. Edward, et al, Grantor; Richard Gibson (Trs.), Grantee; Date of instrument: 28 July 1865; Date of record: 1 Jan. 1866; Book A, Page 117; Kind of instrument: Deed in Trust; Description of property: Part of Cooks Hill Plantation, near Walterboro.

Glover, J. Edward, Grantor; Francis H. Glover, Grantee; Date of instrument: 1 Sept. 1861; Date of record: 16 Jan. 1867; Book A, Page 357; Kind of instrument: Conv. in Fee; Description of property: In Walterboro.

Glover, J. Edward, Grantor; Francis Y. Glover, Grantee; Date of instrument: 15 Mar. 1854; Date of record: 15 Feb. 1867; Book A, Page 400; Kind of instrument: Conv. in Trust; Description of property: Several tracts.

Glover, J. Edward, Grantor; Francis Y. Glover, Grantee; Date of instrument: 10 June 1857; Date of record: 15 Feb. 1867; Book A, Page 404; Kind of instrument: Conv. in Trust; Description of property: In & Near Walterboro.

Glover, J. Edward, Grantor; J. Randall Stanfill, Grantee; Date of instrument: 7 Feb. 1859; Date of record: 23 Mar. 1867; Book A, Page 545; Kind of instrument: T.R.E.; Description of property: Near Walterboro.

Glover, J. Edward, Grantor; Jabez. J. Saunders (Trs.), Grantee; Date of instrument: 22 May 1855; Date of record: 3 Jan. 1884; Book 1, Page 481; Kind of instrument: Conv.; Description of property: In Mashawville.

Glover, J. Edward, Grantor; John Remley, Grantee; Date of instrument: 28 Apr. 1862; Date of record: 27 Nov. 1922; Book 54, Page 97; Kind of instrument: Deed of trust; Description of property: ---.

Glover, J. Edward, Grantor; Paul H. Waring, et al, Grantee; Date of instrument: 20 Jan. 1848; Date of record: 26 Jan. 1867; Book A, Page 330; Kind of instrument: Dec. of Trust; Description of property: ---.

Glover, James S., Grantor; Henry James, Grantee; Date of instrument: 6 Nov. 1863; Date of record: 6 Nov. 1868; Book B, Page 481; Kind of instrument: Title; Description of property: Near Parkers Ferry.

Glover, Jas. S., Grantor; Eliza Glover, Grantee; Date of instrument: 16 Nov. 1857; Date of record: 18 June 1894; Book 14, Page 519; Kind of instrument: T.R.E.; Description of property: In Walterboro.

Glover, Jno. Heyward, Ex'or (by C. E.), Grantor; Maria Glover, Grantee; Date of instrument: 18 Dec. 1846; Date of record: 26 Mar. 1891; Book 10, Page 319; Kind of instrument: T.R.E.; Description of property: Riverplace, et al.

Glover, Jos. Edward, Grantor; John W. Lewis, Grantee; Date of instrument: 28 Feb. 1854; Date of record: 7 Feb. 1870; Book C, Page 496; Kind of instrument: T.R.E.; Description of property: West Side Deer Creek.

Glover, Jos. Edward, Grantor; Jos. Bellinger (Trs.), Grantee; Date of instrument: 7 July 1863; Date of record: 15 Mar. 1867; Book A, Page 459; Kind of instrument: Deed of Marriage Settlement; Description of property: ---.

Glover, Mary E., Grantor; Joseph Bellinger, Grantee; Date of instrument: 9 Mar. 1864; Date of record: 15 Mar. 1867; Book A, Page 462; Kind of instrument: Release of Trusteeship; Description of property: ---.

Goodwin, John, Grantor; A. D. Smoke, Grantee; Date of instrument: 14 Sept. 1861; Date of record: 1 Jan.

1870; Book D, Page 406; Kind of instrument: Title; Description of property: 180 acres on Buckhead Swamp.

Gowan, Wm., et al, Grantor; Geo. Warren (sh'ff), Grantee; Date of instrument: 12 Jan. 1848; Date of record: 14 Apr. 1892; Book 13, Page 225; Kind of instrument: Petition for Title; Description of property: ---.

Gray, Alexander, (Est.), Grantor; Simon Verdier, Grantee; Date of instrument: ---; Date of record: 24 June 1869; Book C, Page 212; Kind of instrument: T. R. E. & Testimony; Description of property: "Cletherall Tract."

Gray, J. W., et al (Ex'or), Grantor; Moses Hodge, Grantee; Date of instrument: 10 Aug. 1860; Date of record: 20 Jan. 1882; Book T, Page 188; Kind of instrument: Conv.; Description of property: Old House Tract, et al.

Gray, James W., (M. E.), Grantor; Benj. Burgh Smith, Grantee; Date of instrument: 1 Nov. 1859; Date of record: 8 June 1869; Book C, Page 180; Kind of instrument: Conv.; Description of property: "Wilderness" on Caw Caw Swamp.

Green, A. D., et al, Grantor; Edwin Walker, Grantee; Date of instrument: 19 Jan. 1857; Date of record: 18 Sept. 1905; Book 27, Page 131; Kind of instrument: Timber sale; Description of property: On Sandy Run and Bull Branch.

Green, A. J., et al, Grantor; Geo. Warren (sh'ff), Grantee; Date of instrument: 12 Jan. 1848; Date of record: 14 Apr. 1892; Book 13, Page 225; Kind of instrument: Petition for Title; Description of property: ---.

Green, J. L., et al, Grantor; Geo. Warren (Sh'ff), Grantee; Date of instrument: 12 Jan. 1848; Date of record: 14 Apr. 1892; Book 13, Page 225; Kind of instrument: Petition for Title; Description of property: ---.

Green, J. W., et al (Trs.), Grantor; Edwin Walker, Grantee; Date of instrument: 19 Jan. 1857; Date of record: 18 Sept. 1905; Book 27, Page 131; Kind of instrument: Timber sale; Description of property: On Sandy Run and Bull Branch.

Green, J. W., et al, Grantor; Edwin Walker, Grantee; Date of instrument: 19 Jan. 1857; Date of record: 18 Sept. 1905; Book 27, Page 131; Kind of instrument: Timber sale; Description of property: On Sandy Run and Bull Branch.

Green, J. W., et al, Grantor; Geo. Warren (Sh'ff), Grantee; Date of instrument: 12 Jan. 1848; Date of record: 14 Apr. 1892; Book 13, Page 225; Kind of instrument: Petition for Title; Description of property: ---.

Green, James, (by Heirs), Grantor; Geo. Warren (Sh'ff), Grantee; Date of instrument: 12 Jan. 1848; Date of record: 14 Apr. 1892; Book 13, Page 225; Kind of instrument: Petition for Title; Description of property: ---.

Green, John L., (by sh'ff), Grantor; H. F. Porter, Grantee; Date of instrument: 10 Jan. 1860; Date of record: 11 Nov. 1912; Book 35, Page 415; Kind of instrument: T.R.E.; Description of property: Salkahatchie River.

Green, John L., Grantor; John Heap, et al, Grantee; Date of instrument: 10 Mar. 1848; Date of record: 14 Apr. 1892; Book 13, Page 275; Kind of instrument: Conv.; Description of property: On Little Salkahatchie Swamp.

Green, L. M., et al, Grantor; Edwin Walker, Grantee; Date of instrument: 19 Jan. 1857; Date of record: 18 Sept. 1905; Book 27, Page 131; Kind of instrument: Timber sale; Description of property: On Sandy Run and Bull Branch.

Green, Larisen, (by Heirs), Grantor; Geo. Warren (sh'ff), Grantee; Date of instrument: 12 Jan. 1848; Date of record: 14 Apr. 1892; Book 13, Page 225; Kind of instrument: Petition for Title; Description of property: ---.

Green, M. R., et al, Grantor; Edwin Walker, Grantee; Date of instrument: 19 Jan. 1857; Date of record:

18 Sept. 1905; Book 27, Page 131; Kind of instrument: Timber sale; Description of property: On Sandy Run and Bull Branch.

Green, T. D., et al, Grantor; Geo. Warren (Sh'ff), Grantee; Date of instrument: 12 Jan. 1848; Date of record: 14 Apr. 1892; Book 13, Page 225; Kind of instrument: Petition for Title; Description of property: ---.

Green, Wm. G., et al, Grantor; Geo. Warren (Sh'ff), Grantee; Date of instrument: 12 Jan. 1848; Date of record: 14 Apr. 1892; Book 13, Page 225; Kind of instrument: Petition for Title; Description of property: ---.

Green, Wm. G., et al, Grantor; Jno. M. Stanfield, Grantee; Date of instrument: 6 Mar. 1854; Date of record: 19 Mar. 1884; Book 2, Page 95; Kind of instrument: T.R.E.; Description of property: On Round O at Irons Cross Roads.

Greenwood, Wm., Grantor; Isaac Minus, Grantee; Date of instrument: 1 Aug. 1810; Date of record: 21 July 1891; Book 11, Page 384; Kind of instrument: T.R.E.; Description of property: On Edisto.

Griffin, L., Grantor; J. W. Griffin, et al, Grantee; Date of instrument: 12 Dec. 1853; Date of record: 31 July 1922; Plat Book, Page 476; Kind of instrument: Plat; Description of property: ---.

Griffith, Ann, (by Trs.), Grantor; S. B. Canady, Grantee; Date of instrument: 9 Dec. 1847; Date of record: 23 Apr. 1885; Book 1, Page 744; Kind of instrument: T.R.E.; Description of property: In Walterboro.

Griffith, Mary, Grantor; Peter Stokes, Grantee; Date of instrument: 30 Apr. 1852; Date of record: 21 May 1869; Book C, Page 169; Kind of instrument: Quit claim; Description of property: Near Smoaks.

Grimball, Isaac, (by C. E.), Grantor; Jasper Rice, Grantee; Date of instrument: 4 Nov. 1850; Date of record: 6 July 1887; Book 6, Page 45; Kind of instrument: T.R.E.; Description of property: On Round O.

Grizelle, Francis, Grantor; Susan Bellinger, Grantee; Date of instrument: Aug. 1844; Date of record: 17 May 1887; Book 5, Page 342; Kind of instrument: Title; Description of property: In Walterboro.

Hagood, Johnson, Grantor; Rizer and Pricher, Grantee; Date of instrument: 2 Nov. 1857; Date of record: 20 Mar. 1873; Book G, Page 275; Kind of instrument: T.R.E.; Description of property: Chauncey Place.

Halford, R. R., Grantor; James Ramsey (Trs.), Grantee; Date of instrument: 20 Dec. 1862; Date of record: 5 Nov. 1866; Book A, Page 288; Kind of instrument: Deed of Gift; Description of property: On Waters of Little Salkahatchie.

Hammond, J. H., (Gar.), Grantor; Emanuel Witsell, Grantee; Date of instrument: 5 Feb. 1844; Date of record: 8 May 1869; Book C, Page 155; Kind of instrument: Grant; Description of property: In Jacksonboro.

Hard, Anna M., et al, Grantor; C. B. Farmer, Grantee; Date of instrument: Sept. 1859; Date of record: 17 June 1869; Book C, Page 196; Kind of instrument: T.R.E.; Description of property: In Walterboro.

Hard, D. W. B., et al, Grantor; C. B. Farmer, Grantee; Date of instrument: Sept. 1859; Date of record: 17 June 1869; Book C, Page 196; Kind of instrument: T.R.E.; Description of property: In Walterboro.

Hard, William I., Grantor; Chas. Baring Farmer, Grantee; Date of instrument: 4 Dec. 1858; Date of record: 17 June 1869; Book C, Page 194; Kind of instrument: Conv.; Description of property: In Walterboro.

Hay, Sam'l H., et al (by C. E.), Grantor; Rizer and Pricher, Grantee; Date of instrument: 2 Nov. 1857; Date of record: 20 Mar. 1873; Book G, Page 275; Kind of instrument: T.R.E.; Description of property: Chauncey Place.

Hayne, I. W., Grantor; Clarence A. Fripp, Grantee; Date of instrument: 1 Sept. 1863; Date of record: 18 Sept. 1866; Book A, Page 190; Kind of instrument: T.R.E.; Description of property: St. Paul's Par.

Hazel, Jno. Ashe, et al (by rec), Grantor; Henry Bischoff, Grantee; Date of instrument: 19 Dec. 1822; Date of record: 15 Jan. 1873; Book G, Page 179; Kind of instrument: T.R.E.; Description of property: On Waters of Pon Pon River.

Henderson, Charlotte M., (Ex'ix), Grantor; Campbell G. Henderson, Grantee; Date of instrument: 25 Apr. 1864; Date of record: 28 July 1866; Book A, Page 145; Kind of instrument: T.R.E.; Description of property: In Walterboro.

Henderson, D. S., (by Ex'ix), Grantor; C. G. Henderson, Grantee; Date of instrument: 25 Apr. 1864; Date of record: 28 July 1866; Book A, Page 145; Kind of instrument: T.R.E.; Description of property: In Walterboro.

Henderson, E. R., Grantor; W. P. Sloman, et al, Grantee; Date of instrument: 1 Mar. 1861; Date of record: 19 Jan. 1906; Book 26, Page 146; Kind of instrument: T.R.E.; Description of property: Bounded by Heyward, et al.

Herndon, J. L., Grantor; Joseph C. Padgett, Grantee; Date of instrument: 8 Dec. 1863; Date of record: 14

Jan. 1884; Book 1, Page 525; Kind of instrument: Conv.; Description of property: Warren Township.

Herndon, P. W. C., Grantor; Laura A. Hiott, Grantee; Date of instrument: 9 Feb. 1800; Date of record: 9 Feb. 1887; Book 5, Page 189; Kind of instrument: T.R.E.; Description of property: Verdier Township.

Heyward, Baynard C., Grantor; Duncan C. Heyward, Grantee; Date of instrument: 19 Dec. ---; Date of record: 31 Dec. 1889; Book 8, Page 287; Kind of instrument: T.R.E.; Description of property: On Black Creek.

Heyward, Betsy, et al, Grantor; T. E. McGeer, Grantee; Date of instrument: 16 Apr. ---; Date of record: 20 May 1907; Book 29, Page 379; Kind of instrument: T.R.E.; Description of property: South by Zion Church.

Heyward, E. R., Grantor; W. P. Sloman, et al, Grantee; Date of instrument: 1 Mar. 1861; Date of record: 19 Jan. 1906; Book 26, Page 146; Kind of instrument: T.R.E.; Description of property: Bounded by Heyward, et al.

Heyward, Esther, et al, Grantor; C. & S. R. R. Co., Grantee; Date of instrument: 6 Dec. 1859; Date of record: 24 Nov. 1916; Book 43, Page 520;

Kind of instrument: Conv.; Description of property: ---.

Heyward, Hannah, (by Ex'or), Grantor; Register of Mesne Conveyance, Colleton Co., Grantee; Date of instrument: 26 Sept. 1839; Date of record: 10 June 1910; Book 28, Page 587; Kind of instrument: Letter of atty.; Description of property: ---.

Heyward, James B., et al, Grantor; W. B. Heyward, et al, Grantee; Date of instrument: 17 July 1861; Date of record: 8 Jan. 1872; Book E, Page 390; Kind of instrument: Indenture; Description of property: St. Bar. Parish.

Heyward, James B., Grantor; Nathaniel Heyward, Grantee; Date of instrument: 5 June 1851; Date of record: 2 June 1884; Book 2, Page 191; Kind of instrument: Release; Description of property: On Cambahee River.

Heyward, M. H., et al, Grantor; W. B. Heyward, et al, Grantee; Date of instrument: 17 July 1861; Date of record: 8 Jan. 1872; Book E, Page 390; Kind of instrument: Indenture; Description of property: St. Bar. Parish.

Heyward, Nathaniel C., Grantor; Wm. C. Heyward, Grantee; Date of instrument: 2 Apr. 1836; Date of record: 10 June 1910; Book 34, Page 208; Kind of instrument: Conv.; Description of property: On Combahee River.

Heyward, Nathaniel, ex or, Grantor; Register of Mesne Conveyance, Colleton County, Grantee; Date of instrument: 26 Sept. 1839; Date of record: 10 June 1910; Book 28, Page 587; Kind of instrument: Letter of atty.; Description of property: ---.

Heyward, Nathaniel, Grantor; Black Creek Baptist Cong., Grantee; Date of instrument: 1 Mar. 1813; Date of record: 2 Apr. 1906; Book 25, Page 82; Kind of instrument: Plat; Description of property: St. Bar. Par.

Heyward, Nathaniel, Grantor; Wm. Loyless, Grantee; Date of instrument: 13 Dec. 1855; Date of record: 7 Aug. 1877; Book J, Page 121; Kind of instrument: Conv.; Description of property: On Orchard Swamp.

Heyward, Thos. S., Grantor; Kittie L. Boykin, et al, Grantee; Date of instrument: 9 Apr. 1861; Date of record: 5 May 1874; Book G, Page 715; Kind of instrument: Marriage settlement; Description of property : ---.

Heyward, Wm. Henry, et al, Grantor; C. & S. R. R. Co., Grantee; Date of instrument: 6 Dec. 1859; Date of record: 24 Nov. 1916; Book 43, Page 520;

Kind of instrument: Conv.; Description of property: ---.

Heyward, Wm., Grantor; Wm. C. Heyward, Grantee; Date of instrument: 16 Feb. 1836; Date of record: 10 June 1910; Book 28, Page 588; Kind of instrument: Conv.; Description of property: On Combahee.

Hickman Edward P., et al, Grantor; Daniel Warren, Grantee; Date of instrument: 28 Dec. 1858; Date of record: 21 Dec. 1883; Book 1, Page 472; Kind of instrument: T.R.E.; Description of property: East by Jones Swamp.

Hickman, Ann, et al, Grantor; Daniel Warren, Grantee; Date of instrument: 28 Dec. 1858; Date of record: 21 Dec. 1883; Book 1, Page 472; Kind of instrument: T.R.E.; Description of property: East by Jones Swamp.

Hiers, C. R., et al, Grantor; James D. Smoke, Grantee; Date of instrument: 7 Apr. 1864; Date of record: 1 Nov. 1869; Book C, Page 328; Kind of instrument: Conv.; Description of property: 150 acres, St. Bar. Parish.

Hiers, G. W., Grantor; R. W. Furman, Grantee; Date of instrument: 7 Oct. 1859; Date of record: 21 Jan. 1868; Book B, Page 114; Kind of instrument: Deed; Description of property: Near Little Salkahatchie.

Hiers, Richard J., et al, Grantor; Joel Padgett, Grantee; Date of instrument: 22 Nov. 1865; Date of record: 23 Sept. 1885; Book 1, Page 798; Kind of instrument: Deed; Description of property: Near Little Salkahatchie.

Hiers, Solomon, Grantor; Doctors Creek Church, Grantee; Date of instrument: --- 1861; Date of record: 12 Apr. 1886; Book 3, Page 345; Kind of instrument: T.R.E.; Description of property: On Doctors Creek.

Hiers, Solomon, Grantor; Wm. D. Jordan, Grantee; Date of instrument: 29 Nov. 1862; Date of record: 25 Jan. 1869; Book B, Page 586; Kind of instrument: Title; Description of property: Between Jones Swamp and Wolf Creek.

Hiers, W. J., et al, Grantor; James D. Smoke, Grantee; Date of instrument: 7 Apr. 1864; Date of record: 1 Nov. 1869; Book C, Page 328; Kind of instrument: Conv.; Description of property: 150 acres, St. Bar. Parish.

Hightower, John, et al, Grantor; Sheba Walker, Grantee; Date of instrument: 25 Mar. 1820; Date of record: 25 Nov. 1873; Book G, Page 560; Kind of instrument: T.R.E.; Description of property: Between Little Salkahatchie and Williams Swamp.

Hill, Wm. B., Grantor; John O. Jaques, Grantee; Date of instrument: 9 Feb. 1861; Date of record: 16 Mar. 1888; Book 6, Page 241; Kind of instrument: T.R.E.; Description of property: Glover Township.

Hiott, C. M., Grantor; John W. Robertson, Grantee; Date of instrument: 23 Sept. 1858; Date of record: 25 Feb. 1903; Plat Book, Page 39; Kind of instrument: Plat; Description of property: ---.

Hiott, Thos. I. D., Grantor; Sarah E. Crosby, Grantee; Date of instrument: 14 Sept. 1859; Date of record: 15 Aug. 1866; Book A, Page 174; Kind of instrument: T.R.E.; Description of property: On White Oak Swamp Head Waters of Horse Shoe.

Hiott, W. C., Grantor; Josiah Hiott, Grantee; Date of instrument: 15 July 1854; Date of record: 15 Dec. 1923; Book 55, Page 409; Kind of instrument: T.R.E.; Description of property: 340 acres more or less.

Horn, Peter, (ex or), Grantor; Wm. Traxler, Grantee; Date of instrument: 10 Oct. 1860; Date of record: 30 Sept. 1875; Book I, Page 370; Kind of instrument: T.R.E.; Description of property: St. Paul's Parish.

Hudson, Daniel, et al, Grantor; Henry C. Glover, Grantee; Date of instrument: 12 July 1851; Date of record: 12 July 1883; Book 1, Page 269; Kind of instrument: Quit claim; Description of property: On Round O.

Hudson, Daniel, Grantor; C. M. Hiott, Grantee; Date of instrument: 1 Feb. 1863; Date of record: 20 Mar. 1867; Book A, Page 475; Kind of instrument: T.R.E.; Description of property: On Waters of Salkahatchie.

Hudson, [Hutson in orginial record] E. C. C. G. M., Grantor; Edwin Walker, Grantee; Date of instrument: 8 Dec. 1850; Date of record: 15 May 1893; Book 14, Page 134; Kind of instrument: T.R.E.; Description of property: On Little Salkahatchie.

Hudson, [Hutson in orginial record] E. C. C. G. M., Grantor; Jesse Smoak, Grantee; Date of instrument: 21 Apr. 1850; Date of record: 16 May 1893; Book 14, Page 137; Kind of instrument: T.R.E.; Description of property: On Waters of Little Salkahatchie.

Hudson, Edward, et al, Grantor; Henry C. Glover, Grantee; Date of instrument: 12 July 1851; Date of record: 12 July 1883; Book 1, Page 269; Kind of instrument: Quit claim; Description of property: On Round O.

Hyrne, Henry, Sr., Grantor; Henry Laresey (Trs.), Grantee; Date of instrument: 1 Jan. 1846; Date of record: 1 July 1867; Book A, Page 626; Kind of instrument: Trust Deed; Description of property: St. Bar. Parish.

Hyrne, Henry, Sr., Grantor; Henry Larisey (Trs.), Grantee; Date of instrument: 1 Jan. 1846; Date of record: 17 Feb. 1887; Book 4, Page 363; Kind of instrument: Trust Deed; Description of property: St. Bar. Par.

Jackson, Andrew, Grantor; Chas. & Sav. R. R. Co., Grantee; Date of instrument: 6 Aug. 1858; Date of record: 23 Feb. 1909; Book 28, Page 419; Kind of instrument: T.R.E.; Description of property: St. Paul's Parish.

Jackson, Wm., Grantor; Geo. W. Hallman, Grantee; Date of instrument: 28 Oct. 1865; Date of record: 3 May 1872; Book G, Page 12; Kind of instrument: T.R.E.; Description of property: On Black Creek.

Jamison, Mary, et al, Grantor; Josiah Padgett, Grantee; Date of instrument: 11 Feb. 1861; Date of record: 21 Feb. 1887; Book 4, Page 377; Kind of instrument: T.R.E.; Description of property: Near Parker's Ferry.

Jamison, Sam'l M., et al, Grantor; Josiah Padgett, Grantee; Date of instrument: 11 Feb. 1861; Date of record: 21 Feb. 1887; Book 4, Page 377; Kind of instrument: T.R.E.; Description of property: Near Parker's Ferry.

Jamison, Sam'l M., et al, Grantor; Josiah Padgett, Grantee; Date of instrument: 14 Feb. 1861; Date of record: 17 Feb. 1887; Book 5, Page 215; Kind of instrument: T.R.E.; Description of property: Near Parker's Ferry.

Jaques, Martin, et al, Grantor; John M. Stanfield, Grantee; Date of instrument: 6 Mar. 1854; Date of record: 19 Mar. 1884; Book 2, Page 95; Kind of instrument: T.R.E.; Description of property: On Round O at Irons Cross Roads.

Jenkins, Abbai M., et al, Grantor; I. S. K. Bennett, Grantee; Date of instrument: 12 may 1864; Date of record: 8 Mar. 1866; Book A, Page 30; Kind of instrument: Conv.; Description of property: Bennett's Point, et al.

Jenkins, Edward E., et al, Grantor; I. S. K. Bennett, Grantee; Date of instrument: 12 May 1864; Date of record: 8 Mar. 1866; Book A, Page 30; Kind of instrument: Conv.; Description of property: Bennett's Point, et al.

Jenkins, I. D., et al, Grantor; B. B. Sams (Trs.), Grantee; Date of instrument: 21 Jan. 1830; Date of record: 10 June 1867; Book A, Page 614; Kind of instrument: Title; Description of property: St. Paul's Parish.

Jenkins, Lydia M., et al, Grantor; I. S. K. Bennett, Grantee; Date of instrument: 12 May 1864; Date of record: 8 Mar. 1866; Book A, Page 30; Kind of instrument: Conv.; Description of property: Bennett's Point, et al.

Jenkins, Micah, et al, Grantor; I. S. K. Bennett, Grantee; Date of instrument: 12 May 1864; Date of record: 8 Mar. 1866; Book A, Page 30; Kind of instrument: Conv.; Description of property: Bennett's Point, et al.

Jenkins, Micah, Grantor; I. S. K. Bennett, Grantee; Date of instrument: 12 Apr. 1864; Date of record: 8 Mar. 1866; Book A, Page 25; Kind of instrument: Conv.; Description of property: Bennett's Point, et al.

Jenkins, Robt. B., Grantor; R. Press Smith, Grantee; Date of instrument: 4 Jan. 1858; Date of record: 10 June 1890; Book 9, Page 415; Kind of instrument: T.R.E.; Description of property: Deer Island.

Jenkins. John, et al, Grantor; I. S. K. Bennett, Grantee; Date of instrument: 12 May 1864; Date of record: 8 Mar. 1866; Book A, Page 30; Kind of instrument: Conv.; Description of property: Bennett's Point, et al.

Jennings, J. S., Grantor; Wm. Hiott, Grantee; Date of instrument: 20 July 1856; Date of record: 23 Apr. 1906; Book 25, Page 89; Kind of instrument: Plat; Description of property: 26 acres, bounded by Jennings, et al.

Jennings, John S., Grantor; Abraham Bennett, Grantee; Date of instrument: 25 Sept. 1865; Date of record: 26 Apr. 1909; Book 28, Page 472; Kind of instrument: T.R.E.; Description of property: Near Foster Bay.

Jennings, John S., Grantor; Ann Stickland, Grantee; Date of instrument: 30 Apr. 1858; Date of record: 23 Apr. 1906; Book 26, Page 359; Kind of instrument: T.R.E.; Description of property: St. Bar. Parish.

Jennings, John S., Grantor; Henry H. Jennings, Grantee; Date of instrument: 20 Apr. 1854; Date of record: 24 Aug. 1870; Book D, Page 290; Kind of instrument: Title; Description of property: On Island Creek.

Jennings, John S., Grantor; Isham Drawdy, Grantee; Date of instrument: 12 Mar. 1859; Date of record: 10 Feb. 1866; Book A, Page 100; Kind of instrument: T.R.E.; Description of property: 130 acres.

Jennings, John S., Grantor; John E. Meister, Grantee; Date of instrument: 27 Nov. 1865; Date of record: 14 Feb. 1866; Book A, Page 17; Kind of instrument: T.R.E.; Description of property: St. Bar. Parish.

Jennings, John S., Grantor; Molton Ritter, Grantee; Date of instrument: 15 Dec. 1860; Date of record: 27 Jan. 1879; Book J, Page 614; Kind of instrument:

Release; Description of property: On Deep Bottom.

Johnson, Benj., Grantor; George Cling Wassen, Grantee; Date of instrument: 18 Nov. 1856; Date of record: 2 Apr. 1879; Book O, Page 86; Kind of instrument: Title; Description of property: Near Walterboro.

Johnson, James, Grantor; Henry M. Spell (Trs.), Grantee; Date of instrument: 5 Feb. 1845; Date of record: 17 Feb. 1887; Book 4, Page 367; Kind of instrument: T.R.E.; Description of property: Near Parker's Ferry.

Johnston, Benj., Grantor; Henry Costine, Grantee; Date of instrument: 31 Mar. 1852; Date of record: 5 July 1887; Book 6, Page 42; Kind of instrument: T.R.E.; Description of property: St. Bar. Parish, Pine Hill Place.

Johnston, Elizabeth, Grantor; Eleanor S. Johnston, Grantee; Date of instrument: 8 Dec. 1855; Date of record: 15 Jan. 1870; Book C, Page 402; Kind of instrument: T.R.E.; Description of property: Bounded by Williams, et al.

Johnston, Emma E., et al, Grantor; A. J. Gonzales, Grantee; Date of instrument: ---; Date of record: 6 Mar. 1887; Book 5, Page 334; Kind of instrument: Release; Description of property: "Social Hall."

Johnston, Joel James, Grantor; Eleanor S. Johnston, Grantee; Date of instrument: 23 Mar. 1839; Date of record: 15 Jan. 1870; Book C, Page 403; Kind of instrument: T.R.E.; Description of property: On Edisto River.

Johnston, John, et al, Grantor; John L. B. Johnston, Grantee; Date of instrument: 21 Mar. 1836; Date of record: 15 Jan. 1870; Book C, Page 394; Kind of instrument: T.R.E.; Description of property: 132 acres, Bounded by Johnston, et al.

Johnston, John, Grantor; Eleanor S. Johnston, Grantee; Date of instrument: 7 May 1847; Date of record: 15 Jan. 1870; Book C, Page 397; Kind of instrument: T.R.E.; Description of property: 65 acres on Hole Branch.

Johnston, John, Grantor; Joel Jas. Johnston, Grantee; Date of instrument: 4 May 1825; Date of record: 15 Jan. 1870; Book C, Page 396; Kind of instrument: T.R.E.; Description of property: On Brick House Tract.

Johnston, John, Grantor; John L. B. Johnston, Grantee; Date of instrument: 4 May 1825; Date of record: 15 Jan. 1870; Book C, Page 400; Kind of instrument: T.R.E.; Description of property: On Edisto River and Augusta Road.

Johnston, Mary B., et al, Grantor; A. J. Gonzales, Grantee; Date of instrument: ---; Date of record:

6 May 1887; Book 5, Page 334; Kind of instrument: Release; Description of property: "Social Hall."

Johnston, Sarah, et al, Grantor; John L. B. Johnston, Grantee; Date of instrument: 21 Mar. 1836; Date of record: 15 Jan. 1870; Book C, Page 394; Kind of instrument: T.R.E.; Description of property: 132 acres, Bounded by Johnston, et al.

Johnston, W. E., et al, Grantor; A. J. Gonzales, Grantee; Date of instrument: ---; Date of record: 6 May 1887; Book 5, Page 334; Kind of instrument: Release; Description of property: "Social Hall."

Jones, Jos. J., Grantor; Henry O. Carter, Grantee; Date of instrument: 21 Jan. 1842; Date of record: 8 Feb. 1912; Book 36, Page 13; Kind of instrument: T.R.E.; Description of property: On Little Salkahatchie.

Jones, Levicey, et al, Grantor; Geo. Warren (sh'ff), Grantee; Date of instrument: 12 Jan. 1848; Date of record: 14 Apr. 1892; Book 13, Page 225; Kind of instrument: Petition for Title; Description of property: ---.

Kinard, Adam, Grantor; Joseph A. Kinsey, Grantee; Date of instrument: 15 July 1861; Date of record: 2 Oct. 1917; Book 44, Page 289; Kind of instrument: Plat; Description of property: On waters of Little Salkahatchie.

Kinard, Jacob, Grantor; Hiram Fralix, Grantee; Date of instrument: 21 Nov. 1838; Date of record: 14 Dec. 1866; Book A, Page 297; Kind of instrument: T.R.E.; Description of property: On Cross Swamp.

King, H. S., Grantor; Mary W. King, Grantee; Date of instrument: 14 Mar. 1851; Date of record: ---; Book 26, Page 490; Kind of instrument: T.R.E.; Description of property: At Adams Run.

King, Hawkins S., Grantor; Henry C. Glover, Grantee; Date of instrument: 16 Sept. 1864; Date of record: 12 Aug. 1868; Book B, Page 394; Kind of instrument: Conv.; Description of property: "Oakville Tract," et al.

Kinsey, Henry, Grantor; Veletta Padgett, Grantee; Date of instrument: 2 Feb. 1855; Date of record: 10 Dec. 1879; Book O, Page 353; Kind of instrument: Title; Description of property: On Little Salkahatchie.

Kinsey, Henry, Jr., Grantor; Levina Catterton, Grantee; Date of instrument: 23 Nov. 1858; Date of record: 27 Jan. 1889; Book 7, Page 484; Kind of instrument: Conv.; Description of property: Warren Township near Buckhead & Little Salkahatchie.

Kinsey, Henry, Sr., Grantor; George W. Kinsey, Grantee; Date of instrument: 23 Nov. 1858; Date of record: 21 Feb. 1889; Book 7, Page 485; Kind of instrument: Conv.; Description of property: Warren Township near Buckhead & Little Salkahatchie.

Kinsey, Henry, Sr., Grantor; James Kinsey, Jr., Grantee; Date of instrument: 10 Nov. 1856; Date of record: 11 Apr. 1900; Book 19, Page 470; Kind of instrument: T.R.E.; Description of property: St. Bar. Parish.

Kinsey, Henry, Sr.; Grantor; Lewis Kinsey, Jr., Grantee; Date of instrument: 19 Oct. 1858; Date of record: 25 Jan. 1869; Book B, Page 588; Kind of instrument: Title; Description of property: On Salkahatchie River.

Kizer, Henry B., et al, Grantor; A. J. Gonzales, Grantee; Date of instrument: ---; Date of record: 6 May 1887; Book 5, Page 334; Kind of instrument: Release; Description of property: Social Hall.

Kizer, Jacob, et al, Grantor; W. S. Yon, Grantee; Date of instrument: 22 Feb. 1864; Date of record: 3 Feb. 1879; Book J, Page 623; Kind of instrument: Title; Description of property: West side of Island Creek.

Kizer, Jane C., et al, Grantor; W. S. Yon, Grantee; Date of instrument: 22 Feb. 1864; Date of record: 3 Feb. 1879; Book J, Page 623; Kind of instrument:

Title; Description of property: West side of Island Creek.

Koger, Chas. E., Grantor; Jas. H. Koger, Grantee; Date of instrument: 29 Oct. 1851; Date of record: 21 Nov. 1918; Book 47, Page 421; Kind of instrument: T.R.E.; Description of property: 205 acres, more or less.

Koger, James H., Grantor; Simon Verdier, Grantee; Date of instrument: 5 May 1851; Date of record: 24 Feb. 1897; Book 16, Page 554; Kind of instrument: T.R.E.; Description of property: On Ireland Creek.

Larisey, Joel, Grantor; Henry Hill (Trs.), Grantee; Date of instrument: 11 Feb. 1851; Date of record: 14 Dec. 1870; Book D, Page 423; Kind of instrument: Title; Description of property: At Sandy Dam.

Larisey, Joel, Grantor; Jesse Smoak, Grantee; Date of instrument: 1 Nov. 1843; Date of record: 19 Apr. 1909; Book 33, Page 104; Kind of instrument: T.R.E.; Description of property: On Big Salkahatchie.

Larisey, Thomas, Grantor; T. I. O. Hiott, Grantee; Date of instrument: 1 May 1854; Date of record: 15 Aug. 1866; Book A, Page 172; Kind of instrument: T.R.E.; Description of property: On waters of Horse Shoe.

LaRoche, Edward D., (et al), Grantor; I. S. K. Bennett, Grantee; Date of instrument: 12 May 1864; Date of record: 8 Mar. 1866; Book A, Page 30; Kind of instrument: Conv.; Description of property: Bennett's Point, et al.

LaRoche, Elizabeth, (et al), Grantor; I. S. K. Bennett, Grantee; Date of instrument: 12 May 1864; Date of record: 8 Mar. 1866; Book A, Page 30; Kind of instrument: Conv.; Description of property: Bennett's Point, et al.

Lazarus, Marks, Grantor; Chas. Baring, Grantee; Date of instrument: 1 Feb. 1832; Date of record: 5 Apr. 1879; Book O, Page 100; Kind of instrument: Title; Description of property: 72 acres.

Lazarus, Marks, Grantor; Chas. Baring, Grantee; Date of instrument: 1 Feb. 1832; Date of record: 5 Apr. 1879; Book O, Page 96; Kind of instrument: Title; Description of property: St. Paul Par.

Leadbetter, H. Matilda, et al, Grantor; C. Baring Farmer, Grantee; Date of instrument: 20 Aug. 1859; Date of record: 17 June 1869; Book C, Page 195; Kind of instrument: T.R.E.; Description of property: In Walterboro.

Leadbetter, Thos. E., et al, Grantor; C. Baring Farmer, Grantee; Date of instrument: 20 Aug. 1859; Date of record: 17 June 1869; Book C, Page 195; Kind of instrument: T.R.E.; Description of property: In Walterboro.

Lemacks, H. M., Grantor; E. A. Lemacks, Grantee; Date of instrument: 1 Dec. 1859; Date of record: 2 Dec. 1867; Book B, Page 53; Kind of instrument: Title; Description of property: Pine Grove.

Lemacks, J. W., Grantor; E. A. Lemacks, Grantee; Date of instrument: 21 July 1864; Date of record: 8 Apr. 1867; Book A, Page 559; Kind of instrument: T.R.E.; Description of property: On Welch's Creek.

Limehouse, Caroline L., Grantor; Alice A. Limehouse, et al, Grantee; Date of instrument: 1 Nov. 1862; Date of record: 16 Apr. 1880; Book P, Page 657; Kind of instrument: Deed; Description of property: 720 acres.

Limehouse, Thomas R., Grantor; Thomas Limehouse, Grantee; Date of instrument: 1 Nov. 1862; Date of record: 1 Jan. 1867; Book A, Page 371; Kind of instrument: Deed; Description of property: 720 acres.

Linder, I. S., Grantor; Isham Padgett, Grantee; Date of instrument: 30 Jan. 1840; Date of record: 13 July 1915; Book 41, Page 387; Kind of instrument: Plat; Description of property : ---.

Linder, J. K., Grantor; Daniel Warren, Grantee; Date of instrument: 10 May 1856; Date of record: 30 June 1866; Book A, Page 152; Kind of instrument: T.R.E.; Description of property: On Island Creek.

Linder, J. S., Grantor; Seaborn Carter, Grantee; Date of instrument: 3 Oct. 1856; Date of record: 1 Aug. 1891; Book 10, Page 462; Kind of instrument: Conv.; Description of property: On Little Salkahatchie.

Linder, Jacob S., Grantor; Lucy Carter, Grantee; Date of instrument: 21 Dec. 1847; Date of record: 1 Aug. 1891; Book 11, Page 400; Kind of instrument: T.R.E.; Description of property: 106 acres, more or less.

Linder, Lewis E., Grantor; Geo. R. E. Linder, Grantee; Date of instrument: 1846; Date of record: 8 Dec. 1871; Book 19, Page 532; Kind of instrument: T.R.E.; Description of property: On Jones Swamp.

Linder, Lewis E., Grantor; John H. Beach, Grantee; Date of instrument: 27 Dec. 1865; Date of record: 17 Dec. 1878; Book J, Page 569; Kind of instrument: Conv.; Description of property: On Jones Swamp.

Lowndes, Wm., (et al) by M. E., Grantor; S. W. Leith, Grantee; Date of instrument: 1 Feb. 1831; Date of record: 26 May 1870; Book D, Page 153; Kind of instrument: Title; Description of property: On Checkessee Creek.

Lowrey, Isham, (by Ex ix), Grantor; Sam'l Sampson, Grantee; Date of instrument: 2 Aug. 1853; Date of record: 13 July 1883; Book 1, Page 272; Kind of instrument: T.R.E.; Description of property: Horse Shoe Tract, et al.

Lowrey, M. A. R., (ex ix), Grantor; S. Sampson, Grantee; Date of instrument: 2 Aug. 1853; Date of record: 13 July 1883; Book 1, Page 272; Kind of instrument: Title; Description of property: Horse Shoe Tract, et al.

Marshall, John T., Grantor; Thomas Cordray, Grantee; Date of instrument: 13 Jan. 1858; Date of record: 10 June 1867; Book A, Page 607; Kind of instrument: Conv.; Description of property: St. Pauls Par.

Martin, John H., Grantor; J. K. Linder, Grantee; Date of instrument: 25 Apr. 1851; Date of record: 29 Aug. 1866; Book A, Page 175; Kind of instrument: T.R.E.; Description of property: In Walterboro.

Mathews, G. A., Grantor; J. R. Mathews, Grantee; Date of instrument: 11 Jan. 1853; Date of record: 3 Oct. 1873; Book G, Page 503; Kind of instrument: T.R.E.; Description of property: On Pon Pon River.

Mathews, J. F., Grantor; J. R. Mathews, Grantee; Date of instrument: 13 May 1850; Date of record: 2 Oct. 1873; Book G, Page 494; Kind of instrument: T.R.E.; Description of property: On waters of Pon Pon River.

Mathews, J. Raven, Grantor; J. Fraser Mathews, Grantee; Date of instrument: 30 May 1850; Date of record: 3 Oct. 1873; Book G, Page 500; Kind of instrument: T.R.E.; Description of property: On Pon Pon River.

Mathews, William R., Grantor; J. Fraser Mathews, Grantee; Date of instrument: 17 June 1858; Date of record: 3 Oct. 1873; Book G, Page 501; Kind of instrument: T.R.E.; Description of property: "Bear Island Tract".

Matthews, G. A., Grantor; Wm. R. Matthews, Grantee; Date of instrument: 13 May 1850; Date of record: 17 Nov. 1875; Book I, Page 411; Kind of instrument: T.R.E.; Description of property: "Bear Island Tract."

Matthews, Jno. Fraser, Grantor; Wm. R. Matthews, Grantee; Date of instrument: 17 June 1858; Date of record: 17 Nov. 1875; Book I, Page 409; Kind of instrument: Conv. in fee; Description of property: West of Jacksonboro Neck.

Matthews, Jno. Raven, Grantor; Wm. Raven Mathews, Grantee; Date of instrument: 21 June 1852; Date of record: 17 Nov. 1875; Book I, Page 412; Kind of instrument: T.R.E.; Description of property: On Ashepoo River.

Matthews, Wm. R., Grantor; John Raven Mathews, Grantee; Date of instrument: 31 Jan. 1856; Date of record: 17 Nov. 1875; Book I, Page 413; Kind of instrument: T.R.E.; Description of property: Part of "Bear Island Tract".

May, John, (Sh'ff), Grantor; Joseph C. Koger, Grantee; Date of instrument: 5 Apr. 1824; Date of record: 24 Sept. 1870; Book D, Page 335; Kind of instrument: Title; Description of property : ---.

May, R. W., Admr (by C. E.), Grantor; Richard Risher, Grantee; Date of instrument: 1 Mar. 1858; Date of record: 2 Jan. 1912; Book 35, Page 79; Kind of instrument: Title; Description of property: On Edisto River.

McBurney, (Dr.) Hugh, (et al) (by C. E.), Grantor; Wm. Pottell, Grantee; Date of instrument: 1 Jan. 1844; Date of record: 26 Mar. 1886; Book 4, Page 190; Kind of instrument: T.R.E.; Description of property: In Walterboro.

McBurney, Eliza, (et al), Grantor; Simon Verdier, Grantee; Date of instrument: ---; Date of record: 22 June 1870; Book D, Page 201; Kind of instrument: Title; Description of property: Peter Smith Land.

McBurney, Eliza, (et al), Grantor; Simon Verdier, Grantee; Date of instrument: ---; Date of record: 31 May 1869; Book C, Page 238; Kind of instrument: T.R.E.; Description of property: Preston Plantation on Horse Shoe.

McBurney, Eliza, Grantor; Richard Minus, Grantee; Date of instrument: 25 Apr. 1838; Date of record: 21 Sept. 1870; Book D, Page 319; Kind of instrument: Title; Description of property: On Edisto River.

McBurney, Hugh, (et al) (by C.E.), Grantor; Mrs. Jane May, Grantee; Date of instrument: 8 May 1832; Date of record: 17 May 1889; Book 8, Page 102; Kind of instrument: T.R.E.; Description of property: In Walterboro.

McBurney, Hugh, (et al by C. E.), Grantor; Dr. F. Y. Glover, Grantee; Date of instrument: 20 Feb. 1829; Date of record: 12 Dec. 1867; Book B, Page 55; Kind of instrument: Title; Description of property: In Walterboro.

McBurney, Hugh, (et al) (by C. E.), Grantor; C. Anne Fraysse, Grantee; Date of instrument: 1 Jan. 1844; Date of record: 8 Oct. 1900; Book 19, Page 526; Kind of instrument: T.R.E.; Description of property: In Walterboro.

McBurney, Hugh, (et al) (by C.E.), Grantor; Jacob Stevens, Grantee; Date of instrument: 16 Mar.

1829; Date of record: 21 Jan. 1887; Book 5, Page 162; Kind of instrument: T.R.E.; Description of property: In Walterboro.

McCants, L. W., (sh'ff), Grantor; John Henry Behling, Grantee; Date of instrument: 9 Aug. 1858; Date of record: ---; Book F, Page 9; Kind of instrument: Conv.; Description of property: St. Pauls Par.

McCants, L. W., (sh'ff), Grantor; John S. B. Jones, Grantee; Date of instrument: 3 June 1861; Date of record: 31 Jan. 1877; Book I, Page 792; Kind of instrument: T.R.E.; Description of property: Fork Salkahatchie.

McCants, L. W., (sh'ff), Grantor; Lewis O'Bryan, Grantee; Date of instrument: 24 Mar. 1853; Date of record: 17 Feb. 1887; Book 5, Page 208; Kind of instrument: T.R.E.; Description of property: Near Parkers Ferry.

McCants, L. W., (sh'ff), Grantor; O. P. Williams, Grantee; Date of instrument: 5 July 1861; Date of record: 15 Mar. 1880; Book P, Page 152; Kind of instrument: T.R.E.; Description of property: St. Bar. Par.

McCants, L. W., (Sh'ff), Grantor; Sam'l Padgett, Jr., Grantee; Date of instrument: 6 Dec. 1859; Date of record: 10 May 1894; Book 15, Page 482;

Kind of instrument: Conv.; Description of property: Bounded by Verdier & Bedon.

McCants, L. W., (sh'ff), Grantor; Wm. Ferguson, Grantee; Date of instrument: 7 Oct. 1861; Date of record: 9 Aug. 1883; Book 1, Page 308; Kind of instrument: Title; Description of property: On Round O.

McCants, L. W., (Sh'ff), Grantor; Wm. Washington Benton (et al), Grantee; Date of instrument: 6 Dec. 1852; Date of record: 3 Oct. 1870; Book D, Page 345; Kind of instrument: Title; Description of property: On Black Creek.

McCants, L. W., (Sheriff), Grantor; H. F. Porter, Grantee; Date of instrument: 10 Jan. 1860; Date of record: 11 Nov. 1912; Book 35, Page 415; Kind of instrument: T.R.E.; Description of property: South on Salkahatchie River.

McFersion (Heirs), Grantor; B. L. Risher, Grantee; Date of instrument: 14 Feb. 1859; Date of record: 13 Nov. 1905; Plat Book, Page 549; Kind of instrument: Plat; Description of property: ---.

Meade, Geo. Gordon, (assignee), Grantor; Jno. S. Jennings, Grantee; Date of instrument: 7 July 1852; Date of record: 20 Jan. 1881; Book P, Page 385; Kind of instrument: T.R.E.; Description of property: St. Bar. Par.

Meade, Geo., (by assignee), Grantor; John S. Jennings, Grantee; Date of instrument: 7 July 1852; Date of record: 20 Jan. 1881; Book P, Page 385; Kind of instrument: T.R.E.; Description of property: St. Bar. Parish.

Middleton, Thomas, Grantor; Chas. Baring, Grantee; Date of instrument: 15 Mar. 1831; Date of record: 5 Apr. 1879; Book O, Page 93; Kind of instrument: Conv.; Description of property: St. Pauls Par.

Mitchell, John S., (et al by M. E.), Grantor; I. W. Hayne, Grantee; Date of instrument: 5 Apr. 1859; Date of record: 18 Sept. 1866; Book A, Page 189; Kind of instrument: T.R.E.; Description of property: St. Pauls Par.

Mondes, Francis, Grantor; Thos. Lemacks, Grantee; Date of instrument: 14 Feb. 1863; Date of record: 18 July 1870; Book D, Page 227; Kind of instrument: Title; Description of property: St. Pauls Parish.

Moorer, Daniel, (Sh'ff), Grantor; John R. Hiott, Grantee; Date of instrument: 12 Mar. 1836; Date of record: 12 July 1882; Book T, Page 459; Kind of instrument: Title; Description of property: On Jones Swamp.

Moorer, Sarah E., Grantor; B. G. Hyrne, Grantee; Date of instrument: ---; Date of record: 30 Jan. 1911;

Book 37, Page 8; Kind of instrument: Title; Description of property: In Walterboro.

Morrison, Jas. H., Grantor; H. R. West, Grantee; Date of instrument: 21 Aug. 1835; Date of record: 5 July 1887; Book 6, Page 34; Kind of instrument: T.R.E.; Description of property: Bounded by Blake, et al.

Moultrie, Wm., Grantor; John Risher, Grantee; Date of instrument: 23 Apr. 1785; Date of record: 21 Nov. 1924; Book 56, Page 265; Kind of instrument: Conveyance; Description of property: ---.

Murdaugh, J. P., Grantor; J. P. Ponds, Grantee; Date of instrument: 31 Dec. 1836; Date of record: 10 May 1887; Book 4, Page 312; Kind of instrument: T.R.E.; Description of property: Broxton Township.

Murdaugh, L. B., Grantor; Berry Stone, Grantee; Date of instrument: 20 Nov. 1847; Date of record: 21 Mar. 1914; Book 38, Page 581; Kind of instrument: T.R.E.; Description of property : ---.

Murray, Andrew, Grantor; Dan'l S. Henderson (Trs.), Grantee; Date of instrument: 14 Apr. 1847; Date of record: 8 May 1867; Book A, Page 561; Kind of instrument: Deed of Gift; Description of property: On Fish Pond Swamp.

Murray, Wm. C., Grantor; Jane W. Condy, Grantee; Date of instrument: ---; Date of record: 27 Feb. 1873; Book G, Page 246; Kind of instrument: Decree; Description of property: 1300 acres.

Nettles, Annie, Grantor; L. J. Sineath, Grantee; Date of instrument: 30 Dec. 1865; Date of record: 3 Mch. 1866; Book A, Page 97; Kind of instrument: Dower; Description of property: East side Salkahatchie Swamp.

Neyle, H. M., (by heirs), Grantor; G. M. Rivers (Dr.), Trustee, Grantee; Date of instrument: 24 Aug. 1861; Date of record: 24 Aug. 1868; Book B, Page 408; Kind of instrument: T.R.E.; Description of property: On Horse Shoe Savannah.

Neyle, H. M., (et al), Grantor; G. M. Rivers (Dr.), Trustee, Grantee; Date of instrument: 24 Aug. 1861; Date of record: 24 Aug. 1868; Book B, Page 408; Kind of instrument: T.R.E.; Description of property: On Horse Shoe Savannah.

Neyle, Jane, (et al), Grantor; G. M. Rivers (Dr.), Trustee, Grantee; Date of instrument: 24 Aug. 1861; Date of record: 24 Aug. 1868; Book B, Page 408; Kind of instrument: T.R.E.; Description of property: On Horse Shoe Savannah.

Neyle, Mary S., (by Trustees), Grantor; James B. Parker, Grantee; Date of instrument: 30 Oct. 1858; Date of record: 9 June 1877; Book J, Page 82; Kind of instrument: T.R.E.; Description of property: On Jones Swamp.

Nicholls, Joshua, Grantor; D. S. Henderson (Trustee), Grantee; Date of instrument: 24 Dec. 1862; Date of record: 20 July 1868; Book B, Page 366; Kind of instrument: Trust Deed; Description of property: In Walterboro.

O'Bryan, A. F., (Ex or), Grantor; Jacob H. Hall, Grantee; Date of instrument: 1 June 1863; Date of record: 15 Aug. 1866; Book A, Page 167; Kind of instrument: T.R.E.; Description of property: In Walterboro.

O'Bryan, A. F., (Ex or), Grantor; Jno. R. Hiott, Grantee; Date of instrument: 1 June 1863; Date of record: 17 July 1884; Book 2, Page 252; Kind of instrument: T.R.E.; Description of property: In Walterboro.

O'Bryan, A. F., (Ex or), Grantor; Samuel M. Jamison, Grantee; Date of instrument: 11 Feb. 1861; Date of record: 17 Feb. 1887; Book 5, Page 210; Kind of instrument: T.R.E.; Description of property: Near Parkers Ferry.

O'Bryan, A. F., (Ex or), Grantor; W. H. O'Bryan, Grantee; Date of instrument: 13 Apr. 1863; Date of record:

21 Aug. 1868; Book B, Page 419; Kind of instrument: T.R.E.; Description of property: In Walterboro.

O'Bryan, A. F., (Ex or), Grantor; Wm. H. O'Bryan, Grantee; Date of instrument: 13 Apr. 1863; Date of record: 21 Aug. 1868; Book B, Page 415; Kind of instrument: T.R.E.; Description of property: On Round O.

O'Bryan, A. F., (Ex or), Grantor; Wm. R. Tucker, Grantee; Date of instrument: 18 Nov. 1861; Date of record: 18 Dec. 1877; Book J, Page 242; Kind of instrument: T.R.E.; Description of property: 80 acres.

O'Bryan, A. F., Grantor; Eliza O'Bryan, Grantee; Date of instrument: 13 Apr. 1863; Date of record: 7 Mch. 1900; Book 20, Page 48; Kind of instrument: T.R.E.; Description of property: in Walterboro.

O'Bryan, A. F., Grantor; W. H. O'Bryan, Grantee; Date of instrument: 13 Apr. 1863; Date of record: 21 Aug. 1868; Book B, Page 416; Kind of instrument: T.R.E.; Description of property: In Walterboro.

O'Bryan, Dicey, (by Trustees), Grantor; Eliza Glover, Grantee; Date of instrument: 1 May 1856; Date of record: 24 Aug. 1871; Book D, Page 500; Kind of instrument: T.R.E.; Description of property: St. Bar. Par.

O'Bryan, Jane, (et al), Grantor; Stephen P. Templeton, Grantee; Date of instrument: 11 Jan. 1853; Date of record: 10 Apr. 1879; Book O, Page 116; Kind of instrument: Deed; Description of property: On Doctors Creek.

O'Bryan, L. J., Grantor; Jane O'Bryan, Trustee, Grantee; Date of instrument: Oct. 1843; Date of record: 10 Apr. 1879; Book O, Page 115; Kind of instrument: Deed; Description of property: On Doctors Creek.

O'Bryan, Lewis, (by Ex or), Grantor; Eliza O'Bryan, Grantee; Date of instrument: 13 Apr. 1863; Date of record: 7 Mch. 1900; Book 20, Page 48; Kind of instrument: T.R.E.; Description of property: In Walterboro.

O'Bryan, Lewis, (by Ex or), Grantor; Jno. R. Hiott, Grantee; Date of instrument: 1 June 1863; Date of record: 17 July 1884; Book 2, Page 252; Kind of instrument: T.R.E.; Description of property: In Walterboro.

O'Bryan, Lewis, (by Ex or), Grantor; Samuel M. Jamison, Grantee; Date of instrument: 11 Feb. 1861; Date of record: 17 Feb. 1887; Book 5, Page 210; Kind of instrument: T.R.E.; Description of property: Near Parkers Ferry.

O'Bryan, Lewis, (by Ex or), Grantor; W. H. O'Bryan, Grantee; Date of instrument: 13 Apr. 1863; Date of record: 21 Aug. 1868; Book B, Page 416; Kind of instrument: T.R.E.; Description of property: In Walterboro.

O'Bryan, Lewis, (by Ex or), Grantor; W. H. O'Bryan, Grantee; Date of instrument: 13 Apr. 1863; Date of record: 21 Aug. 1868; Book B, Page 419; Kind of instrument: T.R.E.; Description of property: In Walterboro.

O'Bryan, Lewis, (by Ex or), Grantor; Wm. H. O'Bryan, Grantee; Date of instrument: 13 Apr. 1863; Date of record: 21 Aug. 1868; Book B, Page 415; Kind of instrument: T.R.E.; Description of property: On Round O.

O'Bryan, Lewis, (by Ex or), Grantor; Wm. R. Tucker, Grantee; Date of instrument: 18 Nov. 1861; Date of record: 18 Dec. 1877; Book J, Page 242; Kind of instrument: T.R.E.; Description of property: 80 acres.

O'Bryan, Lewis, Grantor; J. W. Roberson, Grantee; Date of instrument: 11 Sept. 1846; Date of record: 25 Feb. 1903; Plat Book, Page 42; Kind of instrument: Plat; Description of property: ---.

O'Bryan, Lewis, Grantor; Jacob H. Hall, Grantee; Date of instrument: 1 June 1863; Date of record: 15 Aug. 1866; Book A, Page 167; Kind of instrument: T.R.E.; Description of property: In Walterboro.

O'Bryan, Lewis, Grantor; Jane Crosby (by Trustee), Grantee; Date of instrument: 1851; Date of record: 26 July 1866; Book A, Page 136; Kind of instrument: T.R.E.; Description of property: On Doctors Creek.

O'Bryan, Lewis, Grantor; Samuel Padgett (Trustee), Grantee; Date of instrument: 1851; Date of record: 26 July 1866; Book A, Page 136; Kind of instrument: T.R.E.; Description of property: On Doctors Creek.

O'Bryan, Lewis, Grantor; Wm. A. Fox, Grantee; Date of instrument: 17 Nov. 1859; Date of record: 19 Apr. 1886; Book 3, Page 354; Kind of instrument: T.R.E.; Description of property: In Walterboro.

O'Bryan, R. S., (et al), Grantor; Stephen P. Templeton, Grantee; Date of instrument: 11 Jan. 1853; Date of record: 10 Apr. 1879; Book O, Page 116; Kind of instrument: Deed; Description of property: On Doctors Creek.

Oswald, Geo. W., Grantor; Peter J. Sires, Grantee; Date of instrument: 30 Apr. 1858; Date of record: 13 Oct. 1870; Book D, Page 363; Kind of instrument: T.R.E.; Description of property: Pon Pon Tract, et al.

Oswald, K., (by Ex ix), Grantor; J. S. Glover, Grantee; Date of instrument: 20 Nov. 1852; Date of record: 20 Dec. 1888; Book 6, Page 583; Kind of instrument: Deed; Description of property: On Round O.

Padgett, Isham, Jr., Grantor; Henry Kicklighter, Grantee; Date of instrument: 16 Dec. 1839; Date of record: 7 Apr. 1906; Book 25, Page 86; Kind of instrument: Deed; Description of property: On Little Swamp.

Padgett, J. G., Grantor; D. L. Redish, Grantee; Date of instrument: 8 Jan. 1865; Date of record: 22 Sep. 1885; Book 1, Page 797; Kind of instrument: Title; Description of property: On Cones Branch.

Padgett, Job, Grantor; Thomas Smith, Grantee; Date of instrument: 19 Nov. 1831; Date of record: 6 June 1868; Book B, Page 308; Kind of instrument: Conv.; Description of property: On Little Swamp.

Padgett, Joel, (et al), Grantor; Daniel Loeb, Grantee; Date of instrument: 16 Sept. 1853; Date of record: 1 Nov. 1869; Book C, Page 309; Kind of instrument: Conv.; Description of property: Near Smoaks.

Padgett, Joel, (et al), Grantor; Daniel Loeb, Grantee; Date of instrument: 26 Sept. 1853; Date of record: 1 Nov. 1869; Book C, Page 311; Kind of instrument: Relinquishment of Dower; Description of property: ---.

Padgett, Katherine, (et al), Grantor; Daniel Loeb, Grantee; Date of instrument: 16 Sept. 1853; Date of record: 1 Nov. 1869; Book C, Page 309; Kind of instrument: Conv.; Description of property: Near Smoaks.

Padgett, Katherine, (et al), Grantor; Daniel Loeb, Grantee; Date of instrument: 26 Sept. 1853; Date of record: 1 Nov. 1869; Book C, Page 311; Kind of instrument: Relinquishment of Dower; Description of property : ---.

Padgett, Samuel, (by Sheriff), Grantor; Robert Padgett, Grantee; Date of instrument: 7 Feb. 1850; Date of record: 29 Apr. 1870; Book D, Page 243; Kind of instrument: Title; Description of property: St. Bar. Par.

Parker, Arthur M., et al, Grantor; A. W. Burnett, Grantee; Date of instrument: 10 Feb. 1854; Date of record: 11 Feb. 1875; Book I, Page 166; Kind of instrument: T.R.E.; Description of property: St. Bar. Par.

Parker, Francis S., et al, Grantor; A. W. Burnett, Grantee; Date of instrument: 10 Feb. 1854; Date of record: 11 Feb. 1875; Book I, Page 166; Kind of instrument: T.R.E.; Description of property: St. Bar. Par.

Parker, Jas. B., Trustee, Grantor; Chas. J. Davis, Grantee; Date of instrument: 22 Dec. 1863; Date of record:

11 Sep. 1877; Book J, Page 153; Kind of instrument: T.R.E.; Description of property: Part Johnson Tract.

Parker, Julia R. Grantor; Haskell Rhett (Trustee), Grantee; Date of instrument: 28 Feb. 1852; Date of record: 27 July 1870; Book D, Page 257; Kind of instrument: Marriage settlement; Description of property: Palmetto on Combahee.

Parker, Little B., et al, Grantor; Sheba Walker, Grantee; Date of instrument: 25 Mch. 1820; Date of record: 25 Nov. 1873; Book G, Page 560; Kind of instrument: T.R.E.; Description of property: Near L. Salkahatchie and Willow Swamp.

Parker, M. H., et al, by Trustee, Grantor; Chas. J. Davis, Grantee; Date of instrument: 22 Dec. 1863; Date of record: 11 Sep. 1877; Book J, Page 153; Kind of instrument: T.R.E.; Description of property: Part Johnson Tract.

Parker, Richard, et al, Grantor; Sheba Walker, Grantee; Date of instrument: 11 Mch. 1820; Date of record: 11 Nov. 1873; Book G, Page 560; Kind of instrument: T.R.E.; Description of property: Near L. Salkahatchie and Willow Swamp.

Patterson, Mary E., et al, Grantor; Thos. M. Peeples, Trustee, Grantee; Date of instrument: 19 Jan. 1856; Date of record: 19 Dec. 1885; Book 4,

Page 19; Kind of instrument: Trust Deed; Description of property: Part Jordan Tract.

Patterson, Mary E., Grantor; Richard O'Bryan, et al, Grantee; Date of instrument: 19 Jan. 1856; Date of record: 19 Dec. 1885; Book 4, Page 20; Kind of instrument: Deed; Description of property: Part Jordan Tract.

Patterson, Simon, et al, Grantor; Rachel O'Bryan (Trustee), Grantee; Date of instrument: 19 Jan. 1856; Date of record: 19 Dec. 1885; Book 4, Page 19; Kind of instrument: T.R.E.; Description of property: ---.

Patterson, Simon, et al, Grantor; Thos. M. Peeples, Trustee, Grantee; Date of instrument: 19 Jan. 1856; Date of record: 19 Dec. 1885; Book 4, Page 19; Kind of instrument: Trust Deed; Description of property: Part Jordan Tract.

Patton, Wm., Trustee, by M. E., Grantor; Chas. Baring, Grantee; Date of instrument: 22 Mch. 1832; Date of record: 5 Apr. 1879; Book O, Page 101; Kind of instrument: T.R.E.; Description of property: St. Pauls Parish.

Paul, James L., Grantor; Sampson L. Paul, Grantee; Date of instrument: Jan. 1858; Date of record: 26 May 1870; Book D, Page 157; Kind of instrument: Conv.; Description of property: In Walterboro, et al.

Paul, Sampson L., (by C. E.) (Adm.), Grantor; Sampson L. Paul, Grantee; Date of instrument: 11 Feb. 1845; Date of record: 26 May 1870; Book D, Page 156; Kind of instrument: Conv.; Description of property: On Horse Shoe Creek.

Pinckney, C., Dr., Grantor; Jno. G. Godley (In Trust), Grantee; Date of instrument: 12 June 1839; Date of record: 20 Jan. 1868; Book B, Page 113; Kind of instrument: T.R.E.; Description of property: On waters Ashepoo River.

Polk, Thos., Grantor; Mary Ponds, Grantee; Date of instrument: 15 Dec. 1853; Date of record: 18 Dec. 1916; Book 43, Page 569; Kind of instrument: Conv.; Description of property: On waters of Little Salkahatchie.

Pottle, Wm., (by Ex or), Grantor; Jas. L. Paul, Grantee; Date of instrument: 7 Feb. 1857; Date of record: 26 May 1886; Book 4, Page 188; Kind of instrument: T.R.E.; Description of property: In Walterboro.

Pottle, Wm., (by Ex or), Grantor; Sampson L. Paul, Grantee; Date of instrument: 6 Jan. 1859; Date of record: 26 May 1886; Book 4, Page 192; Kind of instrument: T.R.E.; Description of property: In Walterboro.

Prescott, D. C., et al, Grantor; Eldred Warren, Grantee; Date of instrument: 17 May 1844; Date of record:

3 Feb. 1877; Book I, Page 789; Kind of instrument: T.R.E.; Description of property: St. Bar. Par.

Price, B. G., Grantor; H. R. Price, Grantee; Date of instrument: 1 Sept. 1865; Date of record: 26 Apr. 1889; Book 8, Page 83; Kind of instrument: T.R.E.; Description of property: On Jones Swamp.

Price, O. B. S., Grantor; J. S. Henderson, Trustee (et al), Grantee; Date of instrument: 18 Sept. 1857; Date of record: 7 July 1873; Book G, Page 401; Kind of instrument: T.R.E.; Description of property: St. Bar. Par.

Pringle, Emma S., et al, Grantor; Wm. M. Smith, Grantee; Date of instrument: 11 Mch. 1848; Date of record: 10 June 1910; Book 34, Page 213; Kind of instrument: T.R.E.; Description of property: "Smithfield," St. Bar. Par.

Pringle, Emma S., et al, Grantor; Wm. M. Smith, Grantee; Date of instrument: 28 Jan. 1847; Date of record: 10 June 1910; Book 34, Page 209; Kind of instrument: T.R.E.; Description of property: On Combahee R..

Pringle, W. Alson, et al, Grantor; Wm. M. Smith, Grantee; Date of instrument: 11 Mch. 1848; Date of record: 10 June 1910; Book 34, Page 213;

Kind of instrument: T.R.E.; Description of property: "Smithfield," St. Bar. Par.

Pringle, W. Alson, et al, Grantor; Wm. M. Smith, Grantee; Date of instrument: 28 Jan. 1847; Date of record: 10 June 1910; Book 34, Page 209; Kind of instrument: T.R.E.; Description of property: On Combahee R.

Proveaux, Archibald, Grantor; G. W. Hiers, Grantee; Date of instrument: 26 Dec. 1865; Date of record: 24 Apr. 1876; Book I, Page 611; Kind of instrument: T.R.E.; Description of property: St. Bar. Par.

Proveaux, Elizabeth, (et al), Grantor; J. M. Warren, Grantee; Date of instrument: 21 Sept. 1865; Date of record: 21 June 1869; Book C, Page 206; Kind of instrument: T.R.E.; Description of property: On Black Creek.

Proveaux, John, (et al), Grantor; J. M. Warren, Grantee; Date of instrument: 21 Sept. 1865; Date of record: 21 June 1869; Book C, Page 206; Kind of instrument: T.R.E.; Description of property: On Black Creek.

Proveaux, Mirion, (et al), Grantor; J. M. Warren, Grantee; Date of instrument: 21 Sept. 1865; Date of record: 21 June 1869; Book C, Page 206; Kind of instrument: T.R.E.; Description of property: On Black Creek.

Proveaux, Sarah, et al, Grantor; J. M. Warren, Grantee; Date of instrument: 21 Sept. 1865; Date of record: 21 June 1869; Book C, Page 206; Kind of instrument: T.R.E.; Description of property: On Black Creek.

Pye, Thos., Grantor; Jno. Remeley (Trustee), Grantee; Date of instrument: 19 Nov. 1847; Date of record: 23 Apr. 1885; Book 1 Page 742; Kind of instrument: T.R.E.; Description of property: In Walterboro.

Ramsey, James, Grantor; David Ramsey, Grantee; Date of instrument: 10 Nov. 1865; Date of record: 17 Nov. 1897; Book 16, Page 789; Kind of instrument: Conv.; Description of property: On L. Salkahatchie.

Ramsey, James, Grantor; David Ramsey, Grantee; Date of instrument: 28 Dec. 1865; Date of record: 17 Nov. 1881; Book T, Page 91; Kind of instrument: T.R.E.; Description of property: On Little Salkahatchie.

Ramsey, James, Grantor; Jno. Ramsey, Grantee; Date of instrument: 28 Dec. 1865; Date of record: 17 Nov. 1897; Book 16, Page 787; Kind of instrument: Conv.; Description of property: On L. Salkahatchie.

Ramsey, James, Grantor; Joseph Ramsey, Grantee; Date of instrument: 28 Dec. 1865; Date of record: 28

Feb. 1870; Book C, Page 504; Kind of instrument: T.R.E.; Description of property: On Little Salkahatchie.

Ramsey, Robt., Grantor; James Ramsey, et al, Grantee; Date of instrument: 28 July 1836; Date of record: 16 Nov. 1897; Book 16, Page 786; Kind of instrument: Release; Description of property: On L. Salkahatchie.

Rentz, Elenor J., et al [Eleanor J. Rentz in original record], Grantor; J. D. Sheider [James S. Shider in the original record], Grantee; Date of instrument: 11 Dec. 1858; Date of record: 20 July 1891; Book 11, Page 381; Kind of instrument: T.R.E.; Description of property: Bounded by Stokes, Minus, et al.

Rentz, Peter, et al, Grantor; J. D. Sheider [James S. Shider in the original record], Grantee; Date of instrument: 11 Dec. 1858; Date of record: 20 July 1891; Book 11, Page 381; Kind of instrument: T.R.E.; Description of property: Bounded by Stokes, Minus, et al.

Rhett, Benj., (Dr.), (et al), Grantor; Haskell Rhett, Trustee, Grantee; Date of instrument: 28 Feb. 1852; Date of record: 27 July 1870; Book D, Page 257; Kind of instrument: Marriage settlement; Description of property: "Palmetto" on Combahee.

Rhett, James M., Grantor; Jnc. W. Lewis, Grantee; Date of instrument: 1 Jan. 1850; Date of record: 7 Feb. 1870; Book C, Page 487; Kind of instrument: T.R.E.; Description of property: On Ashepoo.

Rhett, Sarah C., Grantor; R. B. Rhett, Jr. (Trustee), Grantee; Date of instrument: 1 Jan. 1861; Date of record: 3 Nov. 1868; Book B, Page 470; Kind of instrument: Conv. in fee; Description of property: On Chickessee Creek.

Rhodes, Wm., Grantor; Robt. L. Addison, Grantee; Date of instrument: 14 Apr. 1857; Date of record: 16 July 1884; Book 2, Page 249; Kind of instrument: T.R.E.; Description of property: On Round O.

Rice, David, Dr., Grantor; R. B. Rice, Grantee; Date of instrument: 20 Apr. 1839; Date of record: 15 Apr. 1914; Book 40, Page 57; Kind of instrument: Title; Description of property: ---.

Rice, Henry W., Grantor; Richard B. Rice, Grantee; Date of instrument: 10 Feb. 1842; Date of record: 15 Apr. 1914; Book 41, Page 4; Kind of instrument: T.R.E.; Description of property: ---.

Rice, R. J., et al, Grantor; J. Q. A. DuBois, Grantee; Date of instrument: 21 Mch. 1860; Date of record: 9 Nov. 1869; Book C, Page 268; Kind of instrument: Conv.; Description of property: In fork of Salkahatchie.

Rice, Richard B., et al, Grantor; J. Q. A. DuBois, Grantee; Date of instrument: 21 Mch. 1860; Date of record: 9 Nov. 1869; Book C, Page 268; Kind of instrument: Conv.; Description of property: In fork at Salkahatchie.

Riker, D., et al, Grantor; Jas. Rabb, Grantee; Date of instrument: 4 Jan. 1860; Date of record: 20 May 1887; Book 6, Page 20; Kind of instrument: T.R.E.; Description of property: Adams Run Township.

Riker, David, et al, Grantor; Bernard Roddin, Grantee; Date of instrument: 21 Jan. 1864; Date of record: 17 Mch. 1876; Book I, Page 574; Kind of instrument: T.R.E.; Description of property: St. Paul Par.

Riker, David, et al, Grantor; Henry M. Rose, Grantee; Date of instrument: 10 Jan. 1863; Date of record: 2 Sep. 1870; Book D, Page 356; Kind of instrument: T.R.E.; Description of property: Bounded by Riker, et al.

Riker, David, et al, Grantor; Henry Rose, Grantee; Date of instrument: 15 Nov. 1860; Date of record: 2 Sept. 1870; Book D, Page 353; Kind of instrument: T.R.E.; Description of property: In Ravenel.

Riker, David, et al, Grantor; Jno. M. Bryan, Grantee; Date of instrument: 30 Dec. 1864; Date of record: 1

Aug. 1905; Book 27, Page 91; Kind of instrument: T.R.E.; Description of property: St. Paul Par.

Riker, David, et al, Grantor; W. D. H. Kirkwood, Grantee; Date of instrument: 28 Jan. 1860; Date of record: 7 Oct. 1879; Book O, Page 262; Kind of instrument: T.R.E.; Description of property: In Ravenel.

Riker, David, Grantor; Edward Bates, Grantee; Date of instrument: 23 Nov. 1864; Date of record: 18 Sept. 1866; Book A, Page 193; Kind of instrument: T.R.E.; Description of property: St. Paul Par.

Riker, David, Grantor; J. W. Martin, Grantee; Date of instrument: 15 Mch. 1863; Date of record: 21 Mch. 1870; Book D, Page 41; Kind of instrument: Conv. in fee; Description of property: St. Paul Par.

Riker, David, Grantor; Jas. H. Ward, Grantee; Date of instrument: 5 Mch. 1864; Date of record: 9 Aug. 1866; Book A, Page 159; Kind of instrument: T.R.E.; Description of property: St. Paul Par.

Riker, R. H., et al, Grantor; Bernard Rodden, Grantee; Date of instrument: 21 Jan. 1864; Date of record: 17 Mch. 1876; Book I, Page 574; Kind of instrument: T.R.E.; Description of property: St. Paul Par.

Riker, R. H., et al, Grantor; Jas. Rabb, Grantee; Date of instrument: 14 Jan. 1860; Date of record: 20 May 1887; Book 6, Page 20; Kind of instrument: T.R.E.; Description of property: Adams Run Township.

Riker, R. H., Grantor; W. D. H. Kirkwood, Grantee; Date of instrument: 28 Jan. 1860; Date of record: 7 Oct. 1879; Book O, Page 262; Kind of instrument: T.R.E.; Description of property: In Ravenel.

Riker, Robert, et al, Grantor; Jno. M. Bryan, Grantee; Date of instrument: 30 Dec. 1864; Date of record: 1 Aug. 1905; Book 27, Page 91; Kind of instrument: T.R.E.; Description of property: St. Paul Par.

Riker, Robt. H., et al, Grantor; Henry M. Rose, Grantee; Date of instrument: 10 Jan. 1863; Date of record: 2 Sep. 1870; Book D, Page 356; Kind of instrument: T.R.E.; Description of property: Bounded by Riker, et al.

Riker, Robt. H., et al, Grantor; Henry Rose, Grantee; Date of instrument: 15 Nov. 1860; Date of record: 2 Sep. 1870; Book D, Page 353; Kind of instrument: T.R.E.; Description of property: In Ravenel.

Risher, Benj., Grantor; Benj. L. Risher, Grantee; Date of instrument: 14 July 1854; Date of record: 8 July 1910; Book 32, Page 329; Kind of instrument: T.R.E.; Description of property: On Edisto River.

Risher, Benj., Grantor; Lawrence B. Ackerman, Grantee; Date of instrument: 3 Jan. 1855; Date of record: 24 Sep. 1870; Book D, Page 339; Kind of instrument: Conv.; Description of property: St. Bar. Par.

Risher, Benjamine, Grantor; Sarah Risher, Grantee; Date of instrument: 6 Aug. 1793; Date of record: 21 Nov. 1924; Book 56, Page 266; Kind of instrument: Claim of conv.; Description of property: ---.

Risher, Jas. K., et al, Grantor; Jnc. M. Stanfield, Grantee; Date of instrument: 6 Mch. 1854; Date of record: 19 Mch. 1884; Book 2, Page 95; Kind of instrument: T.R.E.; Description of property: At Trans X Road.

Risher, Jno. S., Grantor; J. J. Hutson, Grantee; Date of instrument: 20 Oct. 1850; Date of record: 27 Aug. 1870; Book D, Page 294; Kind of instrument: Conv.; Description of property: On Edisto River.

Risher, Richard, Grantor; H. W. Ackerman, Grantee; Date of instrument: 1 Sep. 1857; Date of record: 24 Sep. 1870; Book D, Page 342; Kind of instrument: Conv.; Description of property: On Horse Pen Bay.

Risher, Richard, Grantor; Sarah Risher, Grantee; Date of instrument: 6 Aug. 1793; Date of record: 21

Nov. 1924; Book 56, Page 266; Kind of instrument: Claim of conv.; Description of property: ---.

Risher, Sarah, Grantor; Richard Risher, Grantee; Date of instrument: 10 Oct. 1794; Date of record: 5 Dec. 1924; Book 56, Page 279; Kind of instrument: Deed; Description of property: Verdier Township.

Rivers, Geo. M., Grantor; Fred Fraser, Trustee, Grantee; Date of instrument: 1 June 1861; Date of record: 22 Jan. 1873; Book G, Page 190; Kind of instrument: T.R.E.; Description of property: In Walterboro.

Rivers, Mallory C., Grantor; F. G. Behre, Grantee; Date of instrument: 7 Oct. 1863; Date of record: 2 Aug. 1866; Book A, Page 151; Kind of instrument: T.R.E.; Description of property: In Walterboro.

Rizer, Christian, et al, Grantor; William Walker, Grantee; Date of instrument: 20 Apr. 1850; Date of record: 16 Dec. 1871; Book E, Page 368; Kind of instrument: T.R.E.; Description of property: On McCunes Branch.

Rizer, Mary, et al, Grantor; William Walker, Grantee; Date of instrument: 20 Apr. 1850; Date of record: 16 Dec. 1871; Book E, Page 368; Kind of instrument: T.R.E.; Description of property: On McCunes Branch.

Robertson, Wm. B., Grantor; Mahala Hiott, Grantee; Date of instrument: 28 Sept. 1838; Date of record: 1 Nov. 1867; Book B, Page 39; Kind of instrument: T.R.E.; Description of property: On Jones Swamp.

Roper, R. W., Grantor; Samuel Smoak, Grantee; Date of instrument: 6 Feb. 1838; Date of record: 17 Apr. 1909; Book 33, Page 106; Kind of instrument: T.R.E.; Description of property: On Big Salkahatchie.

Rose, Jas. L., Grantor; M. M. Freeman, Trustee, Grantee; Date of instrument: 27 July 1855; Date of record: 10 June 1867; Book A, Page 606; Kind of instrument: Conv.; Description of property: St. Paul Par.

Rutherford, Robert, by Master, Grantor; Edward Barnwell, Jr., Grantee; Date of instrument: 28 July 1851; Date of record: 20 Sep. 1874; Book I, Page 20; Kind of instrument: T.R.E.; Description of property: "Hope" Plantation.

Ryan, J. J., Grantor; Dempsey DuBois, Grantee; Date of instrument: 3 Apr. 1861; Date of record: 8 Mch. 1884; Book 1, Page 567; Kind of instrument: Conv.; Description of property: On Salkahatchie.

Ryan, Thos., (Trustee), Grantor; Robt. Fishburne, Grantee; Date of instrument: 10 Nov. 1852; Date of record: 12 Jan. 1875; Book I, Page 474; Kind of instrument: Marriage settlement; Description of property: St. Paul Par.

Sams, B. B., (et al) (by C. E.), Grantor; Richard Freeman, Grantee; Date of instrument: 1 June 1835; Date of record: 10 June 1867; Book A, Page 603; Kind of instrument: Conv. in fee; Description of property: St. Pauls Par.

Sanders, B., Grantor; Jas. Sanders, Grantee; Date of instrument: 3 June 1851; Date of record: 19 Feb. 1912; Book 36, Page 37; Kind of instrument: T.R.E.; Description of property: Bounded by Sauls, et al.

Sanders, Benj., Grantor; Jabez J. Sanders, Grantee; Date of instrument: 1 May 1863; Date of record: 17 Feb. 1883; Book 1, Page 63; Kind of instrument: Title; Description of property: ---.

Sanders, Benj., Grantor; Sarah A. Sanders, Grantee; Date of instrument: 27 July 1847; Date of record: 29 Oct. 1875; Book I, Page 405; Kind of instrument: Plat; Description of property: ---.

Sanders, Burrell, Grantor; Wm. C. Corrie, Grantee; Date of instrument: 11 Aug. 1859; Date of record: 9 Nov. 1909; Book 32, Page 62; Kind of instrument: T.R.E.; Description of property: In Walterboro.

Sanders, Charles S., et al, Grantor; Susan G. Davis, Grantee; Date of instrument: 18 Feb. 1857; Date of record: 9 Apr. 1894; Book 15, Page 463; Kind of instrument: Conv.; Description of property: On Round O.

Sanders, E. B., (et al), Grantor; Susan G. Davis, Grantee; Date of instrument: 18 Feb. 1857; Date of record: 9 Apr. 1894; Book 15, Page 463; Kind of instrument: Conv.; Description of property: On Round O.

Sanders, Jabez J., Grantor; Robert McDermid, Grantee; Date of instrument: 1 Nov. 1863; Date of record: 7 Feb. 1883; Book 1, Page 64; Kind of instrument: Title; Description of property: ---.

Sanders, James, (et al), Grantor; Susan G. Davis, Grantee; Date of instrument: 18 Feb. 1857; Date of record: 9 Apr. 1894; Book 15, Page 463; Kind of instrument: Conv.; Description of property: On Round O.

Sanders, James, Grantor; J. K. Linder, Grantee; Date of instrument: 25 Mar. 1861; Date of record: 29 Aug. 1866; Book A, Page 177; Kind of instrument: T.R.E.; Description of property: On Round O.

Sanders, James, Grantor; Wm. Sanders, Grantee; Date of instrument: 1852; Date of record: 28 Apr. 1892;

Book 13, Page 243; Kind of instrument: Conv.; Description of property: In Walterboro.

Sanders, James, Jr., Grantor; Abraham Willis, Grantee; Date of instrument: 21 Apr. 1852; Date of record: 2 July 1866; Book A, Page 114; Kind of instrument: T.R.E.; Description of property: On Round O.

Sanders, James, Jr., Grantor; Henry Crosby, Grantee; Date of instrument: 11 Jan. 1847; Date of record: 9 Feb. 1886; Book 3, Page 236; Kind of instrument: T.R.E.; Description of property: On Round O.

Sanders, Julia J., by Trustee, Grantor; Robert McDermid, Grantee; Date of instrument: 1 Nov. 1863; Date of record: 3 Jan. 1884; Book 1, Page 482; Kind of instrument: Conv.; Description of property: In Mashaville.

Sanders, Laurence, et al, Grantor; Susan G. Davis, Grantee; Date of instrument: 18 Feb. 1857; Date of record: 9 Apr. 1894; Book 15, Page 463; Kind of instrument: Conv.; Description of property: On Round O.

Sanders, Thomas S., (et al), Grantor; Susan G. Davis, Grantee; Date of instrument: 18 Feb. 1857; Date of record: 9 Apr. 1894; Book 15, Page 463; Kind of instrument: Conv.; Description of property: On Round O.

Sanders, William, (et al), Grantor; Susan G. Davis, Grantee; Date of instrument: 18 Feb. 1857; Date of record: 9 Apr. 1894; Book 15, Page 463; Kind of instrument: Conv.; Description of property: On Round O.

Sanders, William, Grantor; David Gruber, Grantee; Date of instrument: 10 Oct. 1865; Date of record: 10 Feb. 1871; Book E, Page 53; Kind of instrument: Conv.; Description of property: In Walterboro.

Sandford, Mathew, (by Ex or), Grantor; Wm. Traxler, Grantee; Date of instrument: 10 Oct. 1860; Date of record: 30 Sept. 1875; Book I, Page 370; Kind of instrument: T.R.E.; Description of property: St. Paul Parish.

Sauls, Isaac, Grantor; Benj. Sauls, Grantee; Date of instrument: 1 May 1854; Date of record: 10 Dec. 1869; Book C, Page 348; Kind of instrument: Transfer; Description of property: Walnut Hill.

Sauls, Isaac, Grantor; Caleb Sauls, Grantee; Date of instrument: 4 Feb. 1860; Date of record: 25 Apr. 1866; Book A, Page 103; Kind of instrument: T.R.E.; Description of property: Verdier Township.

Scott, B. F., (et al), Grantor; B. B. Sams (Trs.), Grantee; Date of instrument: 21 Jan. 1830; Date of record: 10 June 1867; Book A Page 614; Kind of instrument: Title; Description of property: St. Pauls Parish.

Seabrook, John A., (et al), Grantor; John R. Matthews, Grantee; Date of instrument: ---; Date of record: 2 May 1907; Plat Book, Page 98; Kind of instrument: Plat; Description of property : ---.

Seabrook, John A., (et al), Grantor; John R. Matthews, Grantee; Date of instrument: 30 Jan. 1855; Date of record: 2 May 1907; Book 25, Page 264; Kind Of instrument: Conv.; Description of property: St. Bar. Parish.

Seabrook, John A., Grantor; John R. Matthews, Grantee; Date of instrument: 30 Jan. 1855; Date of record: 2 May 1907; Book 25, Page 267; Kind of instrument: Conv.; Description of property: St. Bar. Parish.

Seabrook, M. M., (et al), Grantor; John R. Matthews, Grantee; Date of instrument: ---; Date of record: 2 May 1907; Plat Book, Page 98; Kind of instrument: Plat; Description of property : ---.

Shepherd, M. E., (et al), Grantor; H. W. Rice, Grantee; Date of instrument: 14 Jan. 1836; Date of record: 18 July 1866; Book A, Page 128; Kind of instrument: Conv. in trust; Description of property : ---.

Simmons, F. Y., Grantor; H. S. King, Grantee; Date of instrument: 10 Jan. 1860; Date of record: 12 Aug. 1868; Book B, Page 391; Kind of instrument: Title; Description of property: St. Pauls Par.

Simmons, Francis Y., Grantor; Hawkins S. King, Grantee; Date of instrument: 4 Jan. 1860; Date of record: 7 Mar. 1879; Book O, Page 59; Kind of instrument: Title; Description of property: St. Pauls Par.

Simmons, Wm., Grantor; F. Y. Simmons, Grantee; Date of instrument: 10 Feb. 1830; Date of record: 12 Aug. 1868; Book B, Page 390; Kind of instrument: Conv.; Description of property: On Toogoodoo Creek.

Simmons, Wm., Grantor; Francis Y. Simmons, Grantee; Date of instrument: 10 Feb. 1830; Date of record: 7 Mar. 1879; Book O, Page 58; Kind of instrument: Conv.; Description of property: On Toogoodoo.

Sineath, B., Grantor; Jos. J. Jones, Grantee; Date of instrument: 20 Oct. 1845; Date of record: 8 Feb. 1912; Book 36, Page 11; Kind of instrument: T.R.E.; Description of property: On Little Salkahatchie.

Smith, Benj., (et al), Grantor; Henry Ramsey, Grantee; Date of instrument: 1 Sept. 1851; Date of record:

6 May 1867; Book A, Page 594; Kind of instrument: Deed; Description of property: On Salkahatchie.

Smith, C. B., Grantor; John Oswald, Grantee; Date of instrument: 20 Feb. 1838; Date of record: 20 Dec. 1888; Book 7, Page 365; Kind of instrument: T.R.E.; Description of property: St. Bar. Parish.

Smith, Elizabeth P., Grantor; J. J. Pringle Smith, et al, Grantee; Date of instrument: 10 Mar. 1848; Date of record: 10 June 1910; Book 34, Page 212; Kind of instrument: Conv.; Description of property :"Smithfield".

Smith, Gideon, (et al), Grantor; H. W. Rice, Grantee; Date of instrument: 14 Jan. 1836; Date of record: 18 July 1866; Book A, Page 128; Kind of instrument: Conv. in trust; Description of property: ---.

Smith, J. J. Pringle, Grantor; Wm. Mason Smith, Grantee; Date of instrument: 1 June 1849; Date of record: 10 June 1910; Book 34, Page 211; Kind of instrument: Conv.; Description of property: Known as "Smithfield".

Smith, R. Press, Grantor; Theodore D. Wagener, Grantee; Date of instrument: 16 Feb. 1864; Date of record: 8 Oct. 1866; Book A, Page 197; Kind of instrument: Conv. in fee; Description of property: Deer Island, et al.

Smith, Sarah, Grantor; Nathan Davis, Grantee; Date of instrument: 3 Feb. 1864; Date of record: 6 June 1868; Book B, Page 310; Kind of instrument: Deed; Description of property: 100 acres.

Smith, Susan P., Grantor; Wm. M. Smith, Grantee; Date of instrument: Feb. 1849; Date of record: 10 June 1910; Book 34, Page 210; Kind of instrument: Conv.; Description of property: Known as "Smithfield".

Smith, Susan, Grantor; Thomas Rumph, Grantee; Date of instrument: 7 Sept. 1857; Date of record: 12 Feb. 1867; Book A, Page 485; Kind of instrument: T.R.E.; Description of property: Near Givhans Ferry.

Smoak, A. J., (et al), Grantor; Levicey Smoak, Grantee; Date of instrument: 9 Nov. 1857; Date of record: 16 Oct. 1882; Book T, Page 547; Kind of instrument: Release; Description of property: ---.

Smoak, Andrew W., Grantor; Riley Kinsey, Grantee; Date of instrument: 21 Jan. 1857; Date of record: 25 Apr. 1888; Book 7, Page 200; Kind of instrument: T.R.E.; Description of property: On Buckhead.

Smoak, Caroline L., (et al), Grantor; Levicey Smoak, Grantee; Date of instrument: 9 Nov. 1857; Date of record: 16 Oct. 1882; Book T, Page 547; Kind of instrument: Release; Description of property: ---.

Smoak, M. S., Grantor; C. J. W. Breland, Grantee; Date of instrument: 17 Jan. 1854; Date of record: 15 Feb. 1890; Book 8, Page 372; Kind of instrument: T.R.E.; Description of property: Bounded by Hoats, Smoak, et al.

Smoak, Margaret, (et al), Grantor; Edwin Walker, Grantee; Date of record: 9 Apr. 1860; Date of record: 8 Sept. 1905; Book 27, Page 112; Kind of instrument: Indenture; Description of property: On Little Salkahatchie.

Smoak, Wm. R., (et al), Grantor; Edwin Walker, Grantee; Date of instrument: 9 Apr. 1860; Date of record: 8 Sept. 1905; Book 27, Page 112; Kind of instrument: Indenture; Description of property: On Little Salkahatchie.

Smoke, James D., Grantor; D. E. Smoke, Grantee; Date of instrument: 8 Jan. 1865; Date of record: 1 Nov. 1869; Book C, Page 327; Kind of instrument: T.R.E.; Description of property: 150 acres bounded by Smith, et al.

Smythe, Ellerson A., (assignee, et al), Grantor; Sam'l Simmons, Grantee; Date of instrument: 19 Feb. ---; Date of record: 19 Apr. 1880; Book P, Page 93; Kind of instrument: T.R.E.; Description of property: Part of Hickory Hill.

Snead, Robt. R., (Trs.), Grantor; Eliza Glover, Grantee; Date of instrument: 1 May 1856; Date of record: 24 Jan. 1871; Book D, Page 500; Kind of instrument: Title; Description of property: 265 acres, St. Bar. Parish.

Snider, John, Grantor; John Heap, Grantee; Date of instrument: 7 Aug. 1849; Date of record: 14 Apr. 1892; Book 13, Page 226; Kind of instrument: Conv.; Description of property: Near Salkahatchie Swamp.

Snider, John, Grantor; John L. Green, Grantee; Date of instrument: 29 Nov. 1844; Date of record: 14 Apr. 1892; Book 13, Page 224; Kind of instrument: Conv.; Description of property: St. Bar. Parish.

Snipes, C. W. C., Grantor; Abram Beach, Grantee; Date of instrument: 9 Aug. 1848; Date of record: 21 Aug. 1868; Book B, Page 413; Kind of instrument: Title; Description of property: On Round O.

Snipes, Susan, (by Trs.), Grantor; Jacob K. Linder, Grantee; Date of instrument: ---; Date of record: 29 Aug. 1866; Book A, Page 176; Kind of instrument: Conv.; Description of property: St. Bar. Parish.

Snipes, Susan, Grantor; Harriett Maree [Harriett Moree in the original record], Grantee; Date of instrument:

22 Feb. 1864; Date of record: 26 Oct. 1874; Book I, Page 47; Kind of instrument: T.R.E.; Description of property: On Round O.

South Carolina, State of, Grantor; Augustus L. Cannon, Grantee; Date of instrument: 7 Apr. 1851; Date of record: 1 Feb. 1910; Book 32, Page 159; Kind of instrument: Deed & Plat; Description of property: Near Orchard Swamp.

South Carolina, State of, Grantor; B. B. Smith, Grantee; Date of instrument: 1 Sept. 1860; Date of record: 1 Feb. 1872; Book F, Page 4; Kind of instrument: Grant; Description of property: St. Pauls Parish.

South Carolina, State of, Grantor; George Warren, Grantee; Date of instrument: ---; Date of record: 25 May 1911; Book 32, Page 498; Kind of instrument: Grant; Description of property: On waters of Little Salkahatchie.

South Carolina, State of, Grantor; George Warren, Grantee; Date of instrument: 17 Dec. 1834; Date of record: 25 May 1911; Plat Book, Page 139; Kind of instrument: Plat; Description of property: On waters of Little Salkahatchie.

South Carolina, State of, Grantor; H. L. Toomer, Grantee; Date of instrument: 3 June 1850; Date of record: 5 May 1877; Book J, Page 72; Kind of instrument: Grant; Description of property: On Ashepoo River, et al.

South Carolina, State of, Grantor; Jacob Stevens, Grantee; Date of instrument: 4 May 1771; Date of record: 18 July 1870; Book D, Page 228; Kind of instrument: Grant; Description of property: St. Pauls Parish.

South Carolina, State of, Grantor; Joseph J. Ferguson (et al), Grantee; Date of instrument: 6 June 1853; Date of record: 24 Sept. 1870; Book D, Page 330; Kind of instrument: Grant; Description of property: On Deep Creek, waters of Edisto.

South Carolina, State of, Grantor; M. W. Clement, Grantee; Date of instrument: 29 Apr. 1857; Date of record: 1 Feb. 1872; Book F, Page 1; Kind of instrument: Grant; Description of property: 805 99/100 acres, St. Pauls Parish.

South Carolina, State of, Grantor; Martin Jaques (et al), Grantee; Date of instrument: 2 July 1849; Date of record: 26 Nov. 1877; Book J, Page 234; Kind of instrument: Grant; Description of property: On Edisto River.

South Carolina, State of, Grantor; Paul Warren, Grantee; Date of instrument: 4 June 1849; Date of record: 8 Mar. 1877; Book J, Page 27; Kind of instrument: Grant; Description of property: On Buckhead.

South Carolina, State of, Grantor; Peter Pye, Grantee; Date of instrument: 6 July 1835; Date of record:

24 Jan. 1871; Book D, Page 496; Kind of instrument: Grant; Description of property: On Elbow Branch.

South Carolina, State of, Grantor; Peter Pye, Grantee; Date of instrument: 6 July 1835; Date of record: 24 Jan. 1871; Book D, Page 498; Kind of instrument: Grant; Description of property: On Elbow Branch.

Speights, E. M., (et al), Grantor; Thomas McTeer, Grantee; Date of instrument: 27 Nov. 1862; Date of record: 20 July 1882; Book T, Page 480; Kind of instrument: Conv.; Description of property: Known as "Oregon".

Speights, E. M., (et al), Grantor; Thomas McTeer, Grantee; Date of instrument: 27 Nov. 1862; Date of record: 20 July 1882; Book T, Page 481; Kind of instrument: Conv.; Description of property: Part of Chickee Tract.

Speights, Kilbride, (et al) [Killbride Speights in original record], Grantor; Thomas McTeer, Grantee; Date of instrument: 27 Nov. 1862; Date of record: 20 July 1882; Book T, Page 480; Kind of instrument: Conv.; Description of property: Known as "Oregon".

Speights, Kilbride, (et al), Grantor; Thomas McTeer, Grantee; Date of instrument: 27 Nov. 1862; Date of record: 20 July 1882; Book T, Page 481; Kind of instrument: Conv.; Description of property: Part of Chickee Tract.

Spell, Benj., (et al), Grantor; P. McDonald, Grantee; Date of instrument: 2 Mar. 1864; Date of record: 26 June 1866; Book A, Page 108; Kind of instrument: T.R.E.; Description of property: On Edisto River.

Spell, Eliza, (et al), Grantor; P. McDonald, Grantee; Date of instrument: 2 Mar. 1864; Date of record: 26 June 1866; Book A, Page 108; Kind of instrument: T.R.E.; Description of property: On Edisto River.

Spell, Henry T., Grantor; Josiah Padgett, Grantee; Date of instrument: 16 May 1863; Date of record: 17 Feb. 1887; Book 5, Page 213; Kind of instrument: Conv.; Description of property: Near Parkers Ferry.

Spell, Jas. F., (by sh'ff), Grantor; Mary Spell, Grantee; Date of instrument: 7 Apr. 1856; Date of record: 21 Feb. 1887; Book 4, Page 375; Kind of instrument: T.R.E.; Description of property: Near Parkers Ferry.

Spell, Jno. D., (by sh'ff), Grantor; Lewis O'Bryan, Grantee; Date of instrument: 24 Mar. 1853; Date of record: 17 Feb. 1887; Book 5, Page 208; Kind of instrument: T.R.E.; Description of property: Near Parkers Ferry.

Spell, Joel, Grantor; Jno. L. B. Johnston, Grantee; Date of instrument: 3 Feb. 1821; Date of record: 15 Jan. 1870; Book C, Page 399; Kind of instrument: T.R.E.; Description of property: On Edisto River.

Spell, Maria, Grantor; G. W. Hiers, Grantee; Date of instrument: 8 Aug. 1861; Date of record: 24 Apr. 1876; Book I, Page 610; Kind of instrument: T.R.E.; Description of property: Near Buckhead.

Stanfield, Elizabeth, (et al), Grantor; M. S. Crosby, et al, Grantee; Date of instrument: ---; Date of record: 17 Jan. 1874; Book H, Page 152; Kind of instrument: Agm't; Description of property: Est of Jas. Stanfield.

Stanfield, J. M., (et al), Grantor; M. S. Crosby, et al, Grantee; Date of instrument: ---; Date of record: 17 Jan. 1874; Book H, Page 152; Kind of instrument: Agm't; Description of property: Est of Jas. Stanfield.

Stanfield, Martha, Grantor; John Bell, Grantee; Date of instrument: 1 Mar. 1853; Date of record: 8 Sept. 1866; Book A, Page 184; Kind of instrument: T.R.E.; Description of property: East side of Black Creek.

State of South Carolina; Grantor; Peter Loper, Grantee; Date of instrument: 3 Feb. 1806; Date of record: 19 June 1882; Book T, Page 411; Kind of instrument: Copy Grant; Description of property: On Doctors Creek.

Stead, Ellen, (Ex ix), Grantor; Richard Reynolds (Trs.), Grantee; Date of instrument: 30 Mar. 1857; Date of record: 2 Dec. 1867; Book B, Page 50; Kind of instrument: Conv.; Description of property: 215 acres, St. Bar. Parish.

Stead, Jas. S., (by Ex'ir), Grantor; Richard Reynolds (Trs.), Grantee; Date of instrument: 30 Mar. 1857; Date of record: 2 Dec. 1867; Book B, Page 50; Kind of instrument: Conv.; Description of property: 215 acres, St. Bar. Parish.

Stephens, J. Wash, Grantor; H. W. Carson, Grantee; Date of instrument: 3 Dec. 1864; Date of record: 8 Oct. 1900; Book 19, Page 517; Kind of instrument: Conv.; Description of property: Bounded by Stephens, et al.

Stephens, Jacob, Grantor; A. Campbell, Grantee; Date of instrument: 8 Apr. 1839; Date of record: 21 Jan. 1887; Book 5, Page 160; Kind of instrument: Gift; Description of property: In Walterboro.

Stephens, Reuben, (et al), Grantor; Jno. M. Stanfield, Grantee; Date of instrument: 6 Mar. 1854; Date of record: 19 Mar. 1884; Book 2, Page 95; Kind of instrument: T.R.E.; Description of property: On Round O at Irons X Roads.

Stewart, Hansford D., Grantor; Martha A. Stewart, Grantee; Date of instrument: 1 Jan. 1848; Date of record: 22 Nov. 1866; Book A, Page 250; Kind of instrument: T.R.E.; Description of property: Bounded by Williams, et al.

Stokes, A. R., Grantor; Stephen Boynton, Grantee; Date of instrument: 20 Apr. 1863; Date of record: 13 Feb. 1867; Book A, Page 370; Kind of instrument: Deed; Description of property: On Combahee waters.

Stokes, Benj., Grantor; Henry C. Glover, Grantee; Date of instrument: 3 July 1851; Date of record: 12 July 1883; Book 1, Page 268; Kind of instrument: Conv.; Description of property: On Round O.

Stokes, Wm., Grantor; Isaac Minus, Grantee; Date of instrument: 20 May 1827; Date of record: 21 July 1891; Book 11, Page 383; Kind of instrument: T.R.E.; Description of property: 330 acres south side of Edisto.

Strickland, Henry, Grantor; Jesse Campbell, Grantee; Date of instrument: 23 Jan. 1846; Date of record: 12 Aug. 1890; Book 9, Page 491; Kind of instrument: T.R.E.; Description of property: Waters of Little Salkahatchie.

Summers, John W., Grantor; Charles H. Rice, Grantee; Date of instrument: 4 May 1863; Date of record: 12 Feb. 1867; Book A, Page 482; Kind of instrument: Title; Description of property: On Edisto River.

Teasdale, Elizabeth M , et al, Grantor; Jno. H. Croskeys, Grantee; Date of instrument: 2 June 1831; Date of record: 17 Feb. 1887; Book 4, Page 364; Kind of instrument: T.R.E.; Description of property: Manning Tract.

Teasdale, R., et al, Grantor; Jno. H. Crosskeys [Croskeys in the original document], Grantee; Date of instrument: 2 June 1831; Date of record: 17 Feb. 1887; Book 4, Page 364; Kind of instrument: T.R.E.; Description of property: "Manning Tract".

Teasdale, Richard, Grantor; James Johnson, Grantee; Date of instrument: 23 Oct. 1839; Date of record: 17 Feb. 1887; Book 4, Page 366; Kind of instrument: Conv.; in fee; Description of property: Near Parkers Ferry.

Templeton, Stephen P., Grantor; Griffin G. Sanders, Grantee; Date of instrument: 8 Jan. 1855; Date of record: 10 Apr. 1879; Book O, Page 118; Kind of instrument: Title; Description of property: On Doctors Creek.

Thomas, Wiley, (by sh'ff), Grantor; Samuel Padgett, Jr., Grantee; Date of instrument: 6 Dec. 1859; Date of record: 10 May 1894; Book 15, Page 482;

Kind of instrument: T.R.E.; Description of property: Bounded by Verdier, Bedon, et al.

Thomas, William, Grantor; Rebecca Morris, Grantee; Date of instrument: 17 Sept. 1848; Date of record: 22 Mch. 1867; Book A, Page 544; Kind of instrument: T.R.E.; Description of property: Near Willow Swamp.

Touchstone, Henry, et al (by sh'ff), Grantor; Wm. Ferguson, Grantee; Date of instrument: 7 Oct. 1861; Date of record: 9 Aug. 1883; Book 1, Page 308; Kind of instrument: Title; Description of property: On Round O.

Touchstone, John, Sr., Grantor; John Touchstone, Jr., Grantee; Date of instrument: 20 Sept. 1861; Date of record: 21 Sept. 1870; Book D, Page 322; Kind of instrument: Title; Description of property: Bounded by Ackerman, Jaques, et al.

Tracy, Emma Heyward, (by C. E.), Grantor; John Hanckell, Grantee; Date of instrument: 5 June 1863; Date of record: 21 Mch. 1866; Book A, Page 92; Kind of instrument: T.R.E.; Description of property: Several tracts.

Tucker, Jno. W. S., Grantor; Geo. W. Patrick, Grantee; Date of instrument: 14 May 1859; Date of record: 12 Feb. 1910; Book 33, Page 589; Kind of instrument: T.R.E.; Description of property: On Edisto River.

Tupper, James, (M. E.), Grantor; Dan'l H. Silcox, Trustee, Grantee; Date of instrument: 4 Feb. 1858; Date of record: 6 Sept. 1888; Book 6, Page 451; Kind of instrument: T.R.E.; Description of property: Near Jacksonboro.

Tupper, James, (M. E.), Grantor; Edward Barnwell, Jr., Grantee; Date of instrument: 28 July 1851; Date of record: 20 Sept. 1874; Book I, Page 20; Kind of instrument: T.R.E.; Description of property: Hope Plan., St. Bar. Par.

Varn, Daniel D., Grantor; Wm. D. L. Varn, Grantee; Date of instrument: 28 May 1856; Date of record: 2 July 1878; Book J, Page 439; Kind of instrument: Title; Description of property: Part of Ferguson Tract.

Verdier, C. B., (by C. E.) (et al), Grantor; Carlos Tracy, Grantee; Date of instrument: Oct. 1858; Date of record: 30 July 1890; Book 8, Page 497; Kind of instrument: T.R.E.; Description of property: In Walterboro.

Verdier, C. B., (by C. E.) (Exix), Grantor; B. S. Rivers, Grantee; Date of instrument: 11 June 1862; Date of record: 17 July 1882; Book T, Page 727; Kind of instrument: Deed; Description of property: In Walterboro.

Verdier, C. B., (by C. E.), Grantor; Catherine B. Verdier, Grantee; Date of instrument: 4 Jan. 1859; Date of record: 24 Feb. 1897; Book 16, Page 555; Kind of instrument: T.R.E.; Description of property: On Island Creek.

Verdier, C. B., (by C. E.), Grantor; L. M. McCants, Grantee; Date of instrument: 27 Jan. 1859; Date of record: 12 Jan. 1874; Book G, Page 615; Kind of instrument: T.R.E.; Description of property: On Round O Road.

Verdier, C. B., Grantor; G. M. Rivers, Grantee; Date of instrument: 15 May 1861; Date of record: 22 Jan. 1873; Book G, Page 189; Kind of instrument: T.R.E.; Description of property: In Walterboro.

Verdier, C. B., Grantor; M. Hethington, Grantee; Date of instrument: 1 Jan. 1863; Date of record: 19 Apr. 1895; Book 17, Page 2; Kind of instrument: T.R.E.; Description of property: On Island Creek.

Verdier, Catherine B., (by C. E.), Grantor; John Bell, Grantee; Date of instrument: 4 Apr. 1859; Date of record: 3 Jan. 1870; Book C, Page 437; Kind of instrument: T.R.E.; Description of property: Formerly of Harper & Verdier.

Verdier, S., Grantor; E. P. Pinckney, Grantee; Date of instrument: 19 Apr. 1852; Date of record: 9 Mch. 1868; Book B, Page 162; Kind of instrument: Title; Description of property: In Walterboro.

Verdier, S., Grantor; Joseph Glover, Grantee; Date of instrument: Jan. 1839; Date of record: 12 Dec. 1867; Book B, Page 58; Kind of instrument: Plat; Description of property: In Walterboro.

Verdier, Simon J., Grantor; J. Edward Glover, Grantee; Date of instrument: 7 Feb. 1848; Date of record: 15 Feb. 1867; Book A, Page 402; Kind of instrument: T.R.E.; Description of property: St. Bar. Par.

Verdier, Simon, Grantor; E. R. Carter, Grantee; Date of instrument: 3 Feb. 1852; Date of record: 29 June 1892; Book 13, Page 86; Kind of instrument: Conv.; Description of property: Near Walterboro.

Vestry & Church Wardens of St. Bartholomew's Parish, Grantor; St. Judes Episcopal Church, W'boro (by Wardens & Vestry), Grantee; Date of instrument: 25 Oct. 1855; Date of record: 14 May 1889; Book 8, Page 97; Kind of instrument: T.R.E.; Description of property: In Walterboro.

Walker, David, (et al), Grantor; William Walker, Grantee; Date of instrument: 20 Apr. 1850; Date of record: 16 Dec. 1871; Book E, Page 368; Kind of instrument: Title; Description of property: On McCuens Branch.

Walker, Edwin, Grantor; Jesse Smoak, Grantee; Date of instrument: 6 Nov. 1861; Date of record: 15 May 1893; Book 14, Page 135; Kind of instrument:

Conv.; Description of property: On Waters Little Salkahatchie.

Walker, Edwin, Grantor; Wm. R. Smoak, et al, Grantee; Date of instrument: 9 Apr. 1860; Date of record: 8 Sept. 1905; Book 27, Page 112; Kind of instrument: Indenture; Description of property: On Little Salkahatchie.

Walker, Geo., (et al), Grantor; Sheba Walker, Grantee; Date of instrument: 25 Mch. 1820; Date of record: 25 Nov. 1873; Book G, Page 560; Kind of instrument: Title; Description of property: Near Willow & Salkahatchie Swamp.

Walker, Geo., et al, Grantor; Joseph P. Carter, Grantee; Date of instrument: 2 Nov. 1865; Date of record: 27 Dec. 1867; Book B, Page 75; Kind of instrument: Title; Description of property: St. Bar. Par.

Walker, Isham, (et al), Grantor; Sheba Walker, Grantee; Date of instrument: 25 Mch. 1820; Date of record: 25 Nov. 1873; Book G, Page 560; Kind of instrument: Title; Description of property: Near Willow & Salkahatchie Swamp.

Walker, Isham, (et al), Grantor; Sheba Walker, Grantee; Date of instrument: 25 Mch. 1820; Date of record: 25 Nov. 1873; Book G, Page 560; Kind of instrument: Title; Description of property: Near Willow & Salkahatchie Swamp.

Walker, Isham, Grantor; David Walker, Grantee; Date of instrument: 1 Jan. 1840; Date of record: 1 Jan. 1867; Book A, Page 364; Kind of instrument: Trust deed; Description of property: In fork of Salkahatchie.

Walker, Jas. D., Grantor; Alien Kinsey, Grantee; Date of instrument: 25 Feb. 1861; Date of record: 14 Apr. 1884; Book 2, Page 148; Kind of instrument: Agmt; Description of property: St. Bar. Par.

Walker, William, Grantor; Jacob Folk, Grantee; Date of instrument: 24 Apr. 1850; Date of record: 16 Dec. 1871; Book E, Page 367; Kind of instrument: Title; Description of property: On McCuens Branch.

Walkington, John, Grantor; James S. Stead, Grantee; Date of instrument: 15 Apr. 1833; Date of record: 2 Dec. 1867; Book B, Page 48; Kind of instrument: Title; Description of property: St. Bar. Parish.

Waring, Paul H., (et al), Grantor; J. Edward Glover, Grantee; Date of instrument: Mch. 1854; Date of record: 7 Feb. 1870; Book C, Page 495; Kind of instrument: Declaration; Description of property: ---.

Waring, Sarah W., (et al), Grantor; J. Edward Glover, Grantee; Date of instrument: Mch. 1854; Date of record: 7 Feb. 1870; Book C, Page 495; Kind of instrument: Declaration; Description of property: ---.

Waring, Thos. R., Grantor; George A. Trenholm, Grantee; Date of instrument: 25 Feb. 1864; Date of record: 7 June 1867; Book A, Page 596; Kind of instrument: Conv.; Description of property: Called Sycamore.

Warley, Jacob Grantor; Frederick Fraser, Grantee; Date of instrument 11 May 1838; Date of record: 8 June 1868; Book B, Page 315; Kind of instrument: Title; Description of property: On Horse Shoe Creek.

Warren, Daniel, (et al), Grantor; Eldred Warren, Grantee; Date of instrument: 17 May 1844; Date of record: 3 Feb. 1877; Book I, Page 789; Kind of instrument: T.R.E.; Description of property: St. Bar. Par.

Warren, Daniel, Grantor; Lewis Beach, Grantee; Date of instrument: 1855; Date of record: 18 Feb. 1879; Book O, Page 27; Kind of instrument: T.R.E.; Description of property: Near Jones Swamp.

Warren, Eldred, Grantor; John Warren, Sr., Grantee; Date of instrument: 22 May 1860; Date of record: 21 Jan. 1871; Book E, Page 1; Kind of instrument: Deed; Description of property: On Waters Buckhead.

Warren, Eldred, Grantor; Paul Warren, Grantee; Date of instrument: 18 Feb. 1858; Date of record: 7 June 1879; Book J, Page 639; Kind of instrument: T.R.E.; Description of property: On Buckhead Swamp.

Warren, Geo., (Sh'ff), Grantor; Robert Padgett, Grantee; Date of instrument: 22 Nov. 1848; Date of record: 29 Apr. 1870; Book D, Page 240; Kind of instrument: T.R.E.; Description of property: On Salkahatchie River.

Warren, Geo., (et al), Grantor; Alex B. Stephens, Grantee; Date of instrument: 29 Dec. 1855; Date of record: 8 June 1885; Book 2, Page 650; Kind of instrument: Title; Description of property: St. Bar. Par.

Warren, Geo., (et al), Grantor; Eldred Warren, Grantee; Date of instrument: 17 May 1844; Date of record: 3 Feb. 1877; Book I, Page 789; Kind of instrument: T.R.E.; Description of property: St. Bar. Parish.

Warren, Geo., (Sh'ff), Grantor; J. M. Crosby, Sr., Grantee; Date of instrument: 5 Mch 1855; Date of record 3 Jan. 1870; Book C, Page 423; Kind of instrument: T.R.E.; Description of property: St. Bar. Par.

Warren, Geo., (Sh'ff), Grantor; Mary Spell, Grantee; Date of instrument: 7 Apr. 1856; Date of record: 21

Feb. 1887; Book 4, Page 375; Kind of instrument: T.R.E.; Description of property: Near Parkers Ferry.

Warren, Geo., (Sh'ff), Grantor; Robt. Padgett, Grantee; Date of instrument: 7 Feb. 1850; Date of record: 29 Apr. 1870; Book D, Page 243; Kind of instrument: T.R.E.; Description of property: St. Bar. Parish.

Warren, Geo., Grantor; M. B. Wilber, Grantee; Date of instrument: 2 Sept. 1864; Date of record: 23 June 1866; Book A, Page 106; Kind of instrument: Deed in Trust; Description of property: In Walterboro.

Warren, Geo., Grantor; M. R. Williams, Grantee; Date of instrument: 5 Jan. 1837; Date of record: 16 Sept. 1895; Book 17, Page 104; Kind of instrument: Conv.; Description of property: On old Field Branch.

Warren, Harriett, (et al), Grantor; Eldred Warren, Grantee; Date of instrument: 17 May 1844; Date of record: 3 Feb. 1877; Book I, Page 789; Kind of instrument: T.R.E.; Description of property: St. Bar. Par.

Warren, James M., Grantor; Jno. Proveaux, Grantee; Date of instrument: 21 Sept. 1865; Date of record: 7 Dec. 1871; Book D, Page 479; Kind of instrument: Deed; Description of property: On Black Creek.

Warren, James, (et al), Grantor; Eldred Warren, Grantee; Date of instrument: 17 May 1844; Date of record: 3 Feb. 1877; Book I, Page 789; Kind of instrument: T.R.E.; Description of property: St. Bar. Par.

Warren, Jas., (by C. E.) (et al), Grantor; Daniel Warren, Grantee; Date of instrument: 5 Apr. 1824; Date of record: 8 Mch. 1877; Book J, Page 28; Kind of instrument: T.R.E.; Description of property: On Buckhead.

Warren, Jno. D., Grantor; James Hunter, Grantee; Date of instrument: ---; Date of record: 22 Oct. 1909; Book 32, Page 56; Kind of instrument: Bond for title; Description of property: Near Ruffin.

Warren, Paul, (et al), Grantor; Eldred Warren, Grantee; Date of instrument: 17 May 1844; Date of record: 3 Feb. 1877; Book I, Page 789; Kind of instrument: T.R.E.; Description of property: St. Bar. Par.

Warren, Paul, Grantor; Eldred Warren, Grantee; Date of instrument: 17 Aug. 1853; Date of record: 3 Feb. 1877; Book I, Page 789; Kind of instrument: Release; Description of property: St. Bar. Parish.

Warren, Paul, Grantor; Eldred Warren, Grantee; Date of instrument: 18 Feb. 1858; Date of record: 26 Aug. 1887; Book 5, Page 485; Kind of instrument: Agn't; Description of property: As to boundary.

Warren, Paul, Grantor; Joseph K. Risher, Grantee; Date of instrument: 4 Jan. 1857; Date of record: 22 July 1909; Book 32, Page 36; Kind of instrument: T.R.E.; Description of property: On Waters Buckhead.

Wescoat, Thos. C., (by sh'ff), Grantor; Thos. C. Wescoat, Grantee; Date of instrument: ---; Date of record: 24 Sept. 1874; Book I, Page 29; Kind of instrument: Conv.; Description of property: "Old Blue House".

Wescoat, Wm., Grantor; Luder F. Behling, Grantee; Date of instrument: 27 Jan. 1865; Date of record: 1 Feb. 1872; Book F, Page 11; Kind of instrument: Conv.; Description of property: Part Spring Grove Plan..

Wescoat, Wm., Grantor; Wm. G. Whilden, Trustee, Grantee; Date of instrument: 26 Nov. 1864; Date of record: 25 Apr. 1868; Book B, Page 276; Kind of instrument: Conv. in Trust; Description of property: St. Paul Par.

West, Jane E., (et al), Grantor; A. McB. Peeples, Grantee; Date of instrument: 1 May 1857; Date of record: 5 July 1887; Book 6, Page 34; Kind of instrument:

T.R.E.; Description of property: Red Hill Tract, et al.

West, Stephen M., (by C. E.) (Guardian), Grantor; R. M. Touchstone, Grantee; Date of instrument: Mch. 14, 1846; Date of record: 21 Sept. 1870; Book D, Page 321; Kind of instrument: Title; Description of property: On south side of Edisto River.

West, Wm. C., (et al), Grantor; A. McB. Peeples, Grantee; Date of instrument: 1 May 1857; Date of record: 5 July 1887; Book 6, Page 34; Kind of instrument: T.R.E.; Description of property: Red Hill Tract, et al.

White, Catherine, (et al), Grantor; Martha White, Grantee; Date of instrument: 13 Jan. 1851; Date of record: 9 Jan. 1907; Book 28, Page 93; Kind of instrument: T.R.E.; Description of property: Part A. M. White estate.

White, Duncan M., (et al), Grantor; Martha White, Grantee; Date of instrument: 13 Jan. 1851; Date of record: 9 Jan. 1907; Book 28, Page 93; Kind of instrument: T.R.E.; Description of property: Part A. M. White estate.

White, Margaret, (et al), Grantor; Martha White, Grantee; Date of instrument: 13 Jan. 1851; Date of record: 9 Jan. 1907; Book 28, Page 93; Kind of instrument: T.R.E.; Description of property: Part A. M. White Estate.

White, William, Grantor; Edward H. Bryan, Grantee; Date of instrument: 28 Feb. 1853; Date of record: 15 Oct. 1866; Book A, Page 215; Kind of instrument: T.R.E.; Description of property: On Little Salkahatchie.

Wichman, A., Grantor; A. W. McLean, Grantee; Date of instrument: ---; Date of record: 29 Jan. 1906; Book 27, Page 316; Kind of instrument: T.R.E.; Description of property: Campbell Plan., et al.

Wichman, A., Grantor; A. W. McLean, Grantee; Date of instrument: ---; Date of record: 30 Jan. 1906; Book 27, Page 322; Kind of instrument: T.R.E.; Description of property: In Walterboro.

Wilbern, W., Grantor; A. Campbell, Grantee; Date of instrument: 21 Aug. 1848; Date of record: 12 Dec. 1867; Book B, Page 60; Kind of instrument: Conv.; Description of property: Buckhead Tract.

Williams, Christopher, Grantor; Richard W. Chaplin, Grantee; Date of instrument: 2 May 1856; Date of record: 10 June 1867; Book A, Page 613; Kind of instrument: Conv.; Description of property: St. Paul Par.

Williams, H. M., Grantor; Eldred Spell, Grantee; Date of instrument: 1840; Date of record: 26 May 1906; Book 27, Page 574; Kind of instrument: Release; Description of property: On Edisto River.

Williams, O. P., (by C. E.), Grantor; Isaac Sauls, Grantee; Date of instrument: 4 Oct. 1852; Date of record: ---; Book C, Page 346; Kind of instrument: Conv.; Description of property: Walnut Hill Tract, St. Paul P.

Williams, O. P., (C. E.), Grantor; Jasper Rice, Grantee; Date of instrument: 4 Nov. 1850; Date of record: 6 July 1887; Book 6, Page 45; Kind of instrument: T.R.E.; Description of property: On Round O.

Williams, O. P., (C. E.), Grantor; M. E. Carn, Grantee; Date of instrument: 31 Mch. 1851; Date of record: 31 Aug. 1870; Book D, Page 300; Kind of instrument: Conv.; Description of property: St. Paul Par.

Williams, O. P., Grantor; L. Warner, Grantee; Date of instrument: 1 Jan. 1866; Date of record: 13 Mch. 1867; Book A, Page 444; Kind of instrument: Conv.; Description of property: In Walterboro.

Williams, O. P., Grantor; Lipmann Williams, Grantee; Date of instrument: 22 July 1862; Date of record: 13 Mch. 1867; Book A, Page 446; Kind of instrument: Conv.; Description of property: In Walterboro.

Williams, O. P., Grantor; Wm. L. Campbell, Grantee; Date of instrument: 1 Feb. 1860; Date of record: ---; Book A, Page 686; Kind of instrument:

Conv.; Description of property: On Horse Shoe Savannah.

Willis, Abraham, Grantor; B. G. Willis, Grantee; Date of instrument: 23 Aug. 1865; Date of record: 2 July 1866; Book A, Page 113; Kind of instrument: T.R.E.; Description of property: On Round O.

Willis, Abraham, Grantor; B. G. Willis, Grantee; Date of instrument: 23 Aug. 1865; Date of record: 2 July 1866; Book A, Page 116; Kind of instrument: T.R.E.; Description of property: On Round O.

Willis, Abraham, Grantor; R. Allen Willis, Grantee; Date of instrument: 23 Nov. 1855; Date of record: 8 Dec. 1866; Book A, Page 298; Kind of instrument: T.R.E.; Description of property: Near Round O.

Willis, R. A., Grantor; Catherine E. Valentine, Grantee; Date of instrument: 16 Feb. 1808; Date of record: 3 Nov. 1899; Book 18, Page 360; Kind of instrument: Conv.; Description of property: Sheridan Township.

Wilson, A. B., (et al), Grantor; John Treanor, Grantee; Date of instrument: 6 June 1863; Date of record: 26 June 1917; Book 46, Page 83; Kind of instrument: Deed; Description of property: ---.

Wilson, Abram, Grantor; Henry Clark, Grantee; Date of instrument: 1 July 1859; Date of record: 24 Mch.

1868; Book B, Page 188; Kind of instrument: Deed; Description of property: St. Paul Par.

Wilson, H. H., (et al), Grantor; John Treanor, Grantee; Date of instrument: 6 June 1863; Date of record: 26 June 1917; Book 46, Page 83; Kind of instrument: Deed; Description of property: ---.

Wilson, James, Grantor; Geo. Warren, Grantee; Date of instrument: 2 Sept. 1852; Date of record: 17 Feb. 1909; Book 33, Page 9; Kind of instrument: T.R.E.; Description of property: Bounded by Smyley, Lemacks, et al.

Wilson, R. W., (per heirs), Grantor; John Treanor, Grantee; Date of instrument: 6 June 1863; Date of record: 26 June 1917; Book 46, Page 83; Kind of instrument: Deed; Description of property: ---.

Wilson, S. F. S., (et al), Grantor; John Treanor, Grantee; Date of instrument: 6 June 1863; Date of record: 26 June 1917; Book 46, Page 83; Kind of instrument: Deed; Description of property: ---.

Wilson, S. F., Grantor; R. W. Wilson, Grantee; Date of instrument: 5 Dec. 1854; Date of record: 26 Jan. 1917; Book 46, Page 80; Kind of instrument: Deed; Description of property : ---.

Wilson, St. J. A., (et al), Grantor; John Treanor, Grantee; Date of instrument: 6 June 1863; Date of record:

26 June 1917; Book 46, Page 83; Kind of instrument: Deed; Description of property: ---.

Witsell, Emanuel, (Dr.) (et al), Grantor; G. M. Rivers (Dr.), Trustee, Grantee; Date of instrument: 24 Aug. 1861; Date of record: 24 Aug. 1868; Book B, Page 408; Kind of instrument: Conv.; Description of property: On Horse Shoe Savannah.

Witsell, Emanuel, Grantor; Chas. Baring, Grantee; Date of instrument: 11 Dec. 1855; Date of record: 5 Apr. 1879; Book O, Page 103; Kind of instrument: T.R.E.; Description of property: St. Paul Par.

Witsell, L. J., (et al), Grantor; George Prince, Grantee; Date of instrument: 10 Feb. 1865; Date of record: 28 May 1866; Book A, Page 68; Kind of instrument: Conv.; Description of property: On Round O.

Witsell, Mary S., (et al), Grantor; G. M. Rivers (Dr.) (Trustee), Grantee; Date of instrument: 24 Aug. 1861; Date of record: 24 Aug. 1868; Book B, Page 408; Kind of instrument: Conv.; Description of property: On Horse Shoe Savannah.

Witsell, Walter H., Grantor; Wm. Lowndes, Grantee; Date of instrument: 1 June 1853; Date of record: 27 Jan. 1882; Book T, Page 201; Kind of instrument: Release in Fee; Description of property: On Pon Pon River.

Wright, John, Grantor; James Wright, Grantee; Date of instrument: 10 Nov. 1857; Date of record: 6 Nov. 1871; Book E, Page 346; Kind of instrument: T.R.E.; Description of property: On Black Creek.

Youngblood, G., (et al), Grantor; Jno. W. Burbidge, Grantee; Date of instrument: ---; Date of record: 22 Jan. 1906; Book 27, Page 307; Kind of instrument: Certificate; Description of property: In Walterboro.

Glossary

Admr. - Administrator in the most usual sense of the word is a person to whom letters of administration, that is, an authority to administer the estate of a deceased person, have been granted by the proper court. He resembles an executor, but, being appointed by the court, and not by the deceased, he has to give security for the due administration of the estate, by entering into a bond with sureties, called the administration bond.

C. E. - Court of Equity heard cases for which there was no legal remedy, frequently over the partition of land, slaves, or other property in an estate.

Conv. - Conveyance; an instrument or deed transferring or passing the title to property by a sealed writing.

Conv. in fee - Conveyance in fee; a transfer of property by a sealed writing which imports an absolute inheritance clear of any condition, limitation, or restriction to particular heirs, but descendible to the heirs in general, male or female, lineal or collateral.

Conv. in trust - Conveyance in trust; the transference of property from one person to another of an equitable right or interest in the property distinct from the legal ownership; the transference of a property interest held by one person for the benefit of another.

Dec. of trust - Declaration of trust; the act by which the person who holds the legal title to property or an estate acknowledges and declares that he holds the same in trust for the use of another person or for a certain specified purpose. The name is also used to designate the deed or other writing embodying such a declaration.

Dec. of uses - Declaration of uses.

Deed - Sealed instrument in writing, duly executed and delivered, containing some transfer, bargain, or contract, as in conveyance of real estate.

Deed in trust - An instrument in use in many states, taking the place and serving the uses of a commonlaw mortgage, by which the legal title to real property is placed in one or more trustees, to secure the repayment of a sum of money or the performance of other conditions.

Est. - Estate; a person's property in lands and tenements.

Et al (Latin) - *Et alii* (and others).

Ex ix - Executrix (f.); person appointed by a testator to execute his will.

Ex or - Executor (m.); person appointed by a testator to execute his will.

Ex parte - On or from one side only; used of such legal matters as injunctions, commissions, hearings, and testimony and ordinarily implying a hearing or examination in the presence of or on papers filed by one party and in the absence of and often without notice to the other party.

Grant - A public authority vests title to public land in a private person.

Indenture - An agreement in writing.

Letter of atty. - Letter of attorney.

M. E. - Master of the Court of Equity.

Mesne conveyance - An intermediate conveyance; one occupying an intermediate position in a chain of title between the first grantee and the present holder.

Plat - A plan, map, or chart of a site.

Power of atty. - Power of attorney; an instrument authorizing one to act as the attorney or agent of the person granting it.

Quit claim - An instrument by which some right, title, or claim, which one person has in or to an estate held by himself or another, is released or relinquished by another.

Release - To give up a legal claim.

Sh'ff - Sheriff.

St. Bar. Parish - St. Bartholomew's Parish; one of the two parishes of Colleton County, located north of St. Helen's.

St. Paul's Parish - One of the two parishes of Colleton County, located on the south side of the Stono River to extend to the north side of South Edisto.

Township - Division of a county.

T. R. E. - title to real estate.

Trs. - trustees; persons appointed, or required by law, to execute a trust; one in whom an , estate, interest, or power is vested under an express or implied agreement to administer or exercise it for the benefit or to the use of another.

Grantee Index

A

Ackerman, H. W., 92
Ackerman, Lawrence B., 3, 92
Ackerman, Stephen O., 3
Addison, Robt. L., 88
Ashe, John S., 5, 23

B

Bailey, James, Jr., 5
Bailey, Richard, 5
Baring, Charles, 24
Baring, Chas., 32, 62, 71, 82, 129
Barnwell, Edward, Jr., 94, 114
Bates, Edward, 90
Beach, Abram, 104
Beach, John H., 64
Beach, Lewis, 119
Beach, R. B., 9
Beach, Wesley, 9
Beck, Josiah, 35
Behling, John Henry, 69
Behling, Luder F., 18, 123
Behre, F. G., 93
Bell, John, 27, 109, 115
Bellinger, E. S. P., 3
Bellinger, Jos., 37
Bellinger, Joseph, 37
Bellinger, Susan, 42
Bennett, Abraham, 55
Bennett, I. S. K., 53, 54, 62
Benton, Elijah, 24, 30
Benton, R. W., 8
Benton, Wm. Washington, 8, 70
Bischoff, Henry, 21, 44
Black Creek Baptist Cong., 47
Bootle, T. A., 7
Borck, Moses, 21
Bowman, Jas., 14
Boykin, Kittie L., 47
Boynton, Stephen, 111
Breland, C. J. W., 103
Bryan, E. H., 11
Bryan, Edward H., 11, 125
Bryan, Jno. M., 89, 91
Burbidge, Jno. W., 130
Burnett, A. W., 80

C

C. & S. R. R. Co., 45, 47
Caleb, Edward, 15

Campbell, A., 110, 125
Campbell, Jesse, 111
Campbell, Wm. L., 126
Canady, O. B. T., 16
Canady, S. B., 42
Cannady, O. T., 22
Cannady, S. B., 16
Cannon, Augustus L., 105
Carn, M. E., 4, 126
Carson, H. W., 110
Carter, E. R., 116
Carter, Henry O., 58
Carter, Joseph P., 117
Carter, Lucy, 64
Carter, Seaborn, 64
Carter, William, 9
Carter, William P., 26
Catterton, Levina, 59
Chaplin, R. W., 16, 17, 19, 30, 31
Chaplin, Richard W., 125
Chas. & Sav. R. R. Co., 52
Clark, Henry, 127
Clarkson, T. B., 13
Clement, M. W., 106
Colleton Co., Register of Mesne Conveyance, 46
Colleton County, Register of Mesne Conveyance, 47
Colliers, Edward, 32
Condy, Jane W., 73

Conoly, Dempsey, 17
Corbett, James, 32
Cordray, Thomas, 65
Cordry, David, 34
Corrie, Wm. C., 95
Costine, Henry, 56
Crosby, Henry, 16, 97
Crosby, Henry E., 19
Crosby, I. M., Sr., 20
Crosby, J. M., Sr., 120
Crosby, Jane, 78
Crosby, M. S., 109
Crosby, Sarah E., 50
Croskeys, 112
Croskeys, Jno. H., 112
Crosskeys, Jno. H., 112

D

Davis, C. I., 22, 26
Davis, Chas. J., 80, 81
Davis, Nathan, 102
Davis, Susan G., 96, 97, 98
Doctors Creek Church, 49
Drawdy, Isham, 55
DuBois, Dempsey, 94
DuBois, J. G. A., 32
DuBois, J. Q. A., 88, 89

F

Farmer, C. B., 43

Farmer, C. Baring, 62
Farmer, Chas. Baring, 43
Fender, J. W., 28
Fender, John J., 28
Fenwick, Edward, 23
Ferguson, Joseph J., 106
Ferguson, Priscilla C., 19
Ferguson, Wm., 70, 113
Fishburne, Robt., 95
Folk, Jacob, 118
Fox, Wm. A., 78
Fralix, Hiram, 59
Fraser, Alexander, 23
Fraser, F. W., 30
Fraser, Fred, 93
Fraser, Frederick, 10, 30, 119
Fraser, Joseph, 24
Fraysse, C. Anne, 68
Freeman, M. M., 94
Freeman, Richard, 21, 95
Fripp, Clarence A., 44
Furman, R. W., 48

G

Garris, B. W., 32
Getsinger, J. J., 33
Gibson, H. A., 11
Gibson, Richard, 35
Givens, David, 6, 7
Glover, Edward, 116
Glover, Eliza, 34, 37, 75, 104
Glover, F. Y., 29, 68
Glover, Francis H., 35
Glover, Francis Y., 35
Glover, Henry C., 50, 51, 59, 111
Glover, J. Edward, 33, 34, 118
Glover, J. S., 78
Glover, Jas. S., 24
Glover, Joseph, 116
Glover, Maria, 14, 37
Godley, Jno. G., 83
Gonzales, A. J., 56, 57, 58, 60
Green, J. W., 4
Green, John L., 104
Greenwood, Wm., 33
Griffin, J. W., 41
Grimes, James, 18
Gruber, David, 98
Gwens, Allen, 8

H

Hall, Jacob H., 74, 77
Hallman, Geo. W., 52
Hanckell, John, 27, 113
Harris, Solomon, 21
Hayne, I. W., 71
Hazel, W. C., 10

Hazel, Wm C., 10
Heap, John, 40, 104
Henderson, C. G., 44
Henderson, Campbell G., 44
Henderson, D. S., 74
Henderson, Dan'l S., 72
Henderson, J. S., 84
Hethington, M., 115
Heyward, Duncan C., 45
Heyward, Nathaniel, 46
Heyward, W. B., 46
Heyward, Wm. C., 46, 48
Hickman, Ann, 5
Hickman, J. S., 20
Hiers, G. W., 85, 109
Hiers, Richard, 19
Hill, Henry, 61
Hiott, C. M., 51
Hiott, Jno. R., 74, 76
Hiott, John R., 71
Hiott, Josiah, 50
Hiott, Laura A., 45
Hiott, Mahala, 94
Hiott, T. I. O., 61
Hiott, T. J. D., 10
Hiott, Wm., 54
Hodge, Moses, 16, 38
Hudson, E. C. C. G. M., 8
Hunter, James, 122
Hutson, 51
Hutson, J. J., 92

Hyrne, B. G., 71

J

Jacoby, Gustave, 10
James, Henry, 36
Jamison, Samuel M., 74, 76
Jaques, John O., 50
Jaques, Martin, 106
Jennings, Henry H., 55
Jennings, Jno. S., 70
Jennings, John S., 71
Johnson, Benj., 13
Johnson, James, 112
Johnston, Eleanor S., 56, 57
Johnston, Jno. L. B., 109
Johnston, Joel Jas., 57
Johnston, John L. B., 57, 58
Jones, John S. B., 69
Jones, Jos. J., 100
Jordan, Wm. D., 49

K

Kicklighter, Henry, 79
King, H. S., 100
King, Hawkins S., 100
King, Mary W., 59
Kinsey, Alien, 118

Kinsey, George W., 59
Kinsey, Henry, 32
Kinsey, James, Jr., 60
Kinsey, Joseph A., 58
Kinsey, Lewis, Jr., 60
Kinsey, Riley, 102
Kirkwood, W. D. H., 90, 91
Klein, J. J., 27, 28
Koger, Chas. E., 20
Koger, Jas. H., 61
Koger, Joseph C., 67

L

Laresey, Henry, 51
Larisey, Henry, 52
Larisey, Joel, 31
Leith, S. W., 31, 64
Lemacks, E. A., 63
Lemacks, Thos., 71
Lewis, Jnc. W., 88
Lewis, John W., 37
Limehouse, Alice A., 63
Limehouse, Thomas, 63
Linder, Geo. R. E., 64
Linder, J. K., 65, 96
Linder, Jacob K., 104
Linder, Lewis E., 6
Loeb, Daniel, 79, 80
Loper, Peter, 109
Lowndes, Wm., 129

Lowrey, Isham, 4, 29
Loyless, Wm., 47
Lucken, Henry W., 4
Lynah, James, 13

M

Maree, Harriett, 104
Marsh, C. J. D., 20
Marshall, John T., 23
Martin, J. W., 90
Mathews, J. Fraser, 66
Mathews, J. R., 65, 66
Mathews, John Raven, 67
Mathews, Wm. Raven, 66
Matthews, John R., 99
Matthews, Wm. R., 66
May, Jane, 30, 68
McCants, L. M., 115
McCants, L. W., 13, 27, 28
McCants, Laurence W., 14, 15
McDermid, Robert, 96, 97
McDonald, P., 108
McGeer, T. E., 45
McLean, A. W., 125
McTeer, Thomas, 107
Meister, John E., 55
Miller, George N., 17
Minus, Isaac, 41, 111
Minus, Richard, 68
Moree, Harriett, 104

Morris, Rebecca, 113
Murdaugh, Mary, 7

N

Newton, William, 25
Nix, Wm. H., 19

O

O'Bryan, Eliza, 75, 76
O'Bryan, Jane, 76
O'Bryan, Lewis, 6, 12, 69, 108
O'Bryan, Rachel, 82
O'Bryan, Richard, 82
O'Bryan, W. H., 74, 75, 76, 77
O'Bryan, Wm. H., 75, 77
Oswald, G. W., 15
Oswald, John, 101

P

Padgett, Isham, 63
Padgett, Joel, 17, 49
Padgett, Joseph C., 44
Padgett, Josiah, 52, 53, 108
Padgett, Robert, 20, 80, 120
Padgett, Robt., 121
Padgett, Sam'l, Jr., 69

Padgett, Samuel, 78
Padgett, Samuel, Jr., 112
Padgett, Veletta, 59
Parker, James B., 74
Patrick, Geo. W., 113
Paul, Jas. L., 12, 83
Paul, Sampson L., 12, 14, 82, 83
Peeples, A. McB., 9, 11, 123, 124
Peeples, Thos. M., 81, 82
Pinckney, E. P., 115
Platt, Edmond B., 14
Ponds, J. P., 72
Ponds, Mary, 83
Porter, H. F., 40, 70
Pottell, Wm., 15, 67
Preacher, Mary, 10
Price, H. R., 84
Pricher, 42, 43
Prince, George, 129
Proveaux, Jno., 121
Pye, Peter, 106, 107
Pye, Thomas, 34

R

Rabb, Jas., 89, 91
Ramsey, David, 86
Ramsey, Henry, 100
Ramsey, James, 42, 87
Ramsey, Jno., 86

Ramsey, Joseph, 86
Redish, D. L., 79
Remeley, Jno., 86
Remley, John, 36
Reynolds, Richard, 110
Rhett, Haskell, 81, 87
Rhett, R. B., Jr., 88
Rice, Charles H., 111
Rice, H. W., 99, 101
Rice, Jasper, 42, 126
Rice, R. B., 88
Rice, Richard B., 88
Risher, B. L., 18, 70
Risher, Benj'm L., 24
Risher, Benj. L., 91
Risher, John, 72
Risher, Joseph K., 123
Risher, Richard, 3, 67, 93
Risher, Sarah, 92
Ritter, Molton, 55
Rivers, B. S., 26, 114
Rivers, G. M., 73, 115, 129
Rizer, 42, 43
Roberson, J. W., 77
Robertson, Alexander, 21
Robertson, John W., 50
Rodden, Bernard, 90
Roddin, Bernard, 89
Rose, Henry, 89, 91
Rose, Henry M., 89, 91
Rumph, Thomas, 102

S

Salinas, A. J., 31
Sampson, S., 65
Sampson, Sam'l, 65
Sams, B. B., 53, 98
Sanders, Griffin G., 112
Sanders, Jabez J., 95
Sanders, Jas., 95
Sanders, Sarah A., 95
Sanders, Wm., 96
Sauls, Benj., 98
Sauls, Caleb, 98
Sauls, Isaac, 12, 126
Saunders, Jabez. J., 36
Sav. R. R. Co., 17
Sheider, J. D., 87
Shider, James S., 87
Silcox, Dan'l H., 34, 114
Simmons, F. Y., 100
Simmons, Francis Y., 100
Simmons, Sam'l, 103
Simmons, Thos. Y., 5
Sineath, L. J., 73
Sires, Peter J., 78
Sloman, W. P., 44, 45
Smith, B. B., 105
Smith, Benj. Burgh, 4, 38
Smith, J. J. Pringle, 101
Smith, R. Press, 54
Smith, Thomas, 79

Smith, Wm. M., 84, 85, 102
Smith, Wm. Mason, 101
Smoak, Jesse, 51, 61, 116
Smoak, Levicey, 102
Smoak, Samuel, 94
Smoak, Wm. R., 117
Smoke, A. D., 37
Smoke, D. E., 103
Smoke, David, 13
Smoke, James D., 48, 49
Snipe, Susan, 25
Spell, Eldred, 125
Spell, Henry M., 56
Spell, Mary, 108, 120
Spell, William, 6
St. Judes Episcopal Church, 116
Stanfield, Jnc. M., 92
Stanfield, Jno. M., 12, 41, 110
Stanfield, John M., 53
Stanfill, J. Randall, 36
Stead, James S., 118
Stephens, Alex, 18
Stephens, Alex B., 120
Stevens, Jacob, 29, 68, 106
Stewart, Martha A., 111
Stickland, Ann, 55
Stokes, Chas. S., 30
Stokes, Peter, 23, 25, 42
Stone, Berry, 72

T

Tabor Church, Trustees, 19
Templeton, Stephen P., 76, 78
Thompson, M. S., 21
Toomer, H. L., 105
Touchstone, John, Jr., 113
Touchstone, R. M., 15, 124
Tracy, Carlos, 26, 114
Traxler, Wm., 50, 98
Treanor, John, 127, 128
Trenholm, George A., 119
Tucker, Wm. R., 75, 77

V

Valentine, Catherine E., 127
Varn, Wm. D. L., 114
Varnado, Henry, 33
Vaughn, M. P., 17
Verdier, Catherine B., 114
Verdier, Simon, 29, 38, 61, 67, 68

W

Wagener, Theodore D., 101
Walker, Alfred P., 3
Walker, David, 118

Walker, Edwin, 8, 38, 39, 40, 51, 103
Walker, Sheba, 49, 81, 117
Walker, William, 22, 93, 116
Ward, Jas. H., 90
Waring, Paul H., 36
Warner, L., 126
Warren, Daniel, 29, 48, 64, 122
Warren, Eldred, 83, 119, 120, 121, 122, 123
Warren, Geo., 38, 39, 40, 41, 58, 128
Warren, George, 105
Warren, J. M., 85, 86
Warren, John, Sr., 119
Warren, Paul, 106, 120
Wassen, George Cling, 56
Wescoat, Thos. C., 123
West, H. R., 72
Whilden, Wm. G., 123
White, Martha, 124
Wilber, M. B., 121
Wilkie, William, 26
Williams, Lipmann, 126
Williams, M. R., 121
Williams, O. P., 22, 69
Willis, Abraham, 97
Willis, B. G., 127
Willis, R. Allen, 127
Wilson, R. W., 128

Witsell, Emanuel, 13, 43
Wright, James, 130

Y

Yon, W. S., 60

www.ingramcontent.com/pod-product-compliance
Lightning Source LLC
Chambersburg PA
CBHW050826160426
43192CB00010B/1916